TEACHER'S PET PUBLICATIONS

LITPLAN TEACHER PACK
for
Shiloh
based on the book by
Phyllis Reynolds Naylor

Written by
Marion B. Hoffman

© 1999 Teacher's Pet Publications
All Rights Reserved

This **LitPlan** on Phyllis Reynolds Naylor's **Shiloh**
has been brought to you by Teacher's Pet Publications, Inc.

Copyright Teacher's Pet Publications 1999
11504 Hammock Point
Berlin MD 21811

Only the student materials in this unit plan may be
reproduced. Pages such as worksheets and study
guides may be reproduced for use in the purchaser's
classroom. For any additional copyright questions,
contact Teacher's Pet Publications.

Table of Contents - Shiloh

Introduction	5
Unit Objectives	8
Reading Assignment Sheet	9
Unit Outline	10
Study Questions (Short Answer)	13
Quiz/Study Questions (Multiple Choice)	23
Pre-reading Vocabulary Worksheets	41
Lesson One (Introductory Lesson)	51
Nonfiction Assignment Sheet	57
Writing Assignment #1	53
Writing Assignment #2	56
Writing Assignment #3	68
Extra Writing Assignments/Discussion ?s	71
Unit Tests	77
Unit Resource Materials	107
Vocabulary Resource Materials	123

A Few Notes About the Author
Phyllis Reynolds Naylor

Phyllis Reynolds Naylor is the author of a series of books for young people. She has written over 70 books. Among her titles are **The Agony of Alice; Alice in Rapture, Sort of; All Because I'm Older; Beetles, Lightly Toasted; Maudie in the Middle; One of the Third Grade Thonkers; Reluctantly Alice; The Witch Herself; Witch Water,** and **Witch's Sister.**

Phyllis Reynolds Naylor was born and raised in Indiana. She attended college first in Illinois and then earned a bachelor's degree in psychology from American University in Washington, DC. Currently she lives with her husband, Rex, at their home in Bethesda, Maryland.

When she was still in kindergarten, Naylor wrote her first book, and when she was sixteen, she sold her first story. But she worked as a teacher and an editor until about 1960, when she began writing full time. Even then her first book was for adults.

She sold her first children's book in 1965 and has concentrated on books for young people since. On the inside back cover of **Shiloh** is information about how Naylor chooses her stories. **Shiloh**, for example, was inspired by a dog that Naylor saw during a visit to West Virginia. She thought it was the saddest dog she had ever seen, and she just couldn't get the dog out of her mind after she returned home to Maryland. And so she wrote the story of Marty Preston and the beagle, Shiloh.

Shiloh is an American Library Association Notable Book for Children. It is the 1992 Winner of the Newberry Medal.

Young people might be interested to know that the story of the "real" Shiloh had a happy ending. After her return home from West Virginia, friends of Naylor's wrote that they had found the dog she had seen near the little community of Shiloh, had taken her in, and had named her Clover. The book is thus dedicated to Frank and Trudy Madden and a dog named Clover.

Introduction

This unit has been designed to develop students' reading, writing, thinking, and language skills through exercises and activities related to **Shiloh** by Phyllis Reynolds Naylor. It includes fifteen lessons, supported by extra resource materials.

The **introductory lesson** introduces students to four themes of the novel (personal trust, family responsibility, community values, and the responsibility of pet ownership) through a bulletin board activity. Subsequent lessons focus on the theme of the responsibility of pet ownership.

The **reading assignments** are approximately 18 pages each; some are a little shorter while others are a little longer. Students have approximately 15 minutes of pre-reading work to do prior to each reading assignment. This pre-reading work involves reviewing the study questions for the assignment and doing some vocabulary work for 7 to 10 vocabulary words they will encounter in their reading.

The **study guide questions** are fact-based questions; students can find the answers to these questions right in the text. These questions come in two formats: short answer or multiple choice. The best use of these materials is probably to use the short answer version of the questions as study guides for students since answers will be more complete and to use the multiple choice version for occasional quizzes.

The **vocabulary work** is intended to enrich students' vocabularies as well as to aid in the students' understanding of the book. Prior to each reading assignment, students will complete a two-part worksheet for approximately 7 to 10 vocabulary words in the upcoming reading assignment. Part I focuses on students' use of general knowledge and contextual clues by giving the sentence in which the word appears in the text. Students are then to write down what they think the words mean based on the words' usage. Part II nails down the definitions of the words by giving students dictionary definitions of the words and having students match the words to the correct definitions based on the words' contextual usage. Students should then have an understanding of the words when they meet them in the text.

After each reading assignment, students will go back and formulate answers for the study guide questions. Discussion of these questions serves as a **review** of the most important events and ideas presented in the reading assignments.

After students complete extra discussion questions, there is a **vocabulary review** lesson which pulls together all of the fragmented vocabulary lists for the reading assignments and gives students a review of all of the words they have studied.

Shiloh Introduction page 2

Following the reading of the book, two lessons are devoted to the **extra discussion questions/writing assignments**. These questions focus on interpretation, critical analysis, and personal response, employing a variety of thinking skills and adding to the students' understanding of the novel. These questions may be done as a **group activity**. Using the information they have acquired so far through individual work and class discussions, students may get together to further examine the text and to brainstorm ideas relating to the themes of the novel.

The group activity is followed by a **reports and discussion** session in which the groups share their ideas about the book with the entire class; thus, the entire class gets exposed to many different ideas regarding the themes and events of the book.

There are three **writing assignments** in this unit, each with the purpose of informing, persuading, or expressing personal opinions. The first assignment is to **inform**: students compose a classified ad for a lost dog, cat, or other small animal; for a newborn small animal from a pet shop; or for a newborn or a grown animal from a breeder. This assignment helps students to consider what is involved in acquiring an animal, the choices that people have when they decide to add a pet to their household, and the pluses and minuses of each. It also helps them to learn to craft a classified ad. The second assignment gives students the opportunity to express their **personal ideas**: students decide what kind of animal they wish to acquire and from what source and then go about preparing for the animal to live in their home. The third assignment is to give students a chance to **persuade**: students may support or oppose local leash laws, pet licensing, clean-up ordinances, or pet abuse laws.

In addition, there is a **nonfiction reading assignment**. Students are required to read a piece of nonfiction related in some way to **Shiloh**. After reading their nonfiction pieces, students will fill out a worksheet on which they answer questions regarding facts, interpretation, criticism, and personal opinions. During one class period, students make **oral presentations** about the nonfiction pieces they have read. This not only exposes all students to a wealth of information, but it also gives students the opportunity to practice public speaking.

There is an optional **class project** (Project Animal Rescue) through which students gain first-hand knowledge of the situation of abandoned and otherwise unwanted animals and have some part in helping to do something about this problem.

The **review lesson** pulls together all aspects of the unit. The teacher is given four or five choices of activities or games to use which all serve the same basic function of reviewing all of the information presented in the unit.

The **unit test** comes in four separate formats:
>   matching/short answer/essay/vocabulary (1 test)
>   matching/short answer/quotations/vocabulary (1 test)
>   matching/multiple choice/quotations/vocabulary (2 tests)
>   matching/short answer critical thinking/essay/vocabulary (1 advanced test)

Also in this unit is a **unit resource section** with suggestions for an in-class library, crossword and word search puzzles related to **Shiloh**, and extra vocabulary worksheets. There is a list of **bulletin board ideas** which gives suggestions for bulletin boards to go along with this unit. In addition, there is a list of **extra class activities** the teacher could use to enhance the unit or as a substitution for an exercise the teacher feels is inappropriate for his or her class.

Answer keys are located directly after the **reproducible student materials** throughout the unit. The student materials may be reproduced for use in the teacher's classroom without infringement of copyright. No other portion of this unit may be reproduced without the written consent of Teacher's Pet Publications, Inc.

Unit Objectives - Shiloh

1. Through reading **Shiloh** by Phyllis Reynolds Naylor, students will gain a better understanding of the themes of trust, family responsibility, community values, and the responsibilities of pet ownership. One theme, pet ownership, is focused on specifically.

2. Students will demonstrate their understanding of the text on four levels: factual, interpretive, critical, and personal.

3. Students will define their own viewpoints on the aforementioned themes.

4. Students will be exposed to new ways of looking at the themes above.

5. Students will create a plan for solving some of the problems created by irresponsible pet ownership.

6. Students will practice reading aloud as well as silently.

7. Students will enrich their vocabularies and improve their understanding of the novel through the vocabulary lessons prepared for use in conjunction with it.

8. Students will practice writing through a variety of assignments.

9. The writing assignments in this unit are geared to several purposes:
    a. to check the students' reading comprehension
    b. to make students think about the ideas presented in the book
    c. to allow students to write from personal experience, to inform, and to persuade
    d. to provide the opportunity to review standard English
    e. to encourage critical and logical thinking

10. Students will be encouraged to make connections between the book and real life.

Reading Assignment Sheet - Shiloh

Section of the Text Assigned	Date Assigned	Date to be Completed
Chapters 1 & 2		
Chapters 3 & 4		
Chapters 5 & 6		
Chapters 7 & 8		
Chapters 9 & 10		
Chapters 11 & 12		
Chapters 13, 14, & 15		

Unit Outline - Shiloh

1 Unit overview Introduction Distribution Set up bulletin board activity WA#1 (pers exp)	2 Bulletin board activity WA#2 (inform) NFRA	3 NFRA research WA#2 continued	4 Writing conferences WA#2 revisions	5 NFRA reports
6 Knowledge related to book PVR Ch. 1 & 2	7 Review Ch. 1 & 2 Set up Project Animal Rescue	8 PVR Ch. 3 & 4	9 PVR 5 & 6 Theme discussion	10 PVR Ch. 7 & 8 Theme discussion
11 Language exercise	12 PVR Ch. 9 & 10	13 PVR Ch. 11 & 12 WA#3 (persuade) Project updates	14 PVR Ch. 13, 14, 15 Character, theme, and plot discussion through quotations	15 Main idea discussion with Extra WA/Discussion Questions Project updates Prep for Unit Tests
16 Unit Tests				

P Preview Study Questions
V Vocabulary work
R Reading
WA Writing Assignment

STUDY GUIDE QUESTIONS AND ANSWER KEY

Short Answer Study Questions - Shiloh

Chapters 1 and 2
1. When does Marty Preston first show that he cares about animals?
2. When is Marty's favorite time to go up into the hills?
3. What does Marty find up in the hills in this first chapter?
4. What is Marty's reaction when he sees the beagle dog cringe?
5. Why won't Marty's mother let Marty have a dog?
6. Why does Marty name the dog "Shiloh"?
7. How old are Marty's sisters and what are their names?
8. What does Marty's father say they have to do with the dog?
9. How does Marty's father respond to Marty's complaints about how Judd Travers treats his dogs?
10. What does Judd do to the dog that convinces Marty that he was right to mistrust Judd?

Chapters 3 and 4
1. By the morning after finding the dog, what has Marty decided to do?
2. Why isn't Marty paid for babysitting his two younger sisters?
3. What does Marty think about when he sees his sisters catching lightning bugs and putting them in a jar?
4. Why does Judd say he keeps his dogs lean and mean?
5. What does Judd tell Marty about naming dogs?
6. What dead animal does Marty remember finding up on the ridge?
7. What special financial responsibility do Marty's parents have?
8. What is the first promise that Marty breaks?
9. What promise does Marty make to Shiloh?
10. What does Marty build for Shiloh?

Chapters 5 and 6
1. What three problems does Marty have to solve in this section?
2. What system does Marty create for saving some of his dinner for Shiloh?
3. What lie does Marty tell his parents in order to get out of the house to see Shiloh?
4. Why does Judd visit the Preston family just as Marty returns home?
5. What other dog does Marty tell Judd he has seen?
6. How does Marty rationalize his second lie to Judd Travers?
7. What question does Marty pose to Jesus?
8. Why doesn't Marty want David Howard to visit him?
9. What does Marty start to learn about lying when he tells his parents that there isn't much for David to do on a visit to the Preston house?
10. How old is Marty?

Shiloh Short Answer Study Questions page 2

Chapters 7 and 8
1. What kind of pet does David have and what is its name?
2. When Marty lets Mrs. Howard pack him a second "lunch" to take home with him, what does Marty start to think about lying?
3. Why does Mr. Wallace at the corner store sell Marty some old food at a cheap price?
4. How does Marty justify the lies he keeps telling to people?
5. Why do people on Marty's father's postal route start leaving him more food?
6. When does Marty get his first real chance to play with Shiloh and bring the dog into the house?
7. Why is Marty's mother worried about frown lines?
8. Who finally discovers Marty playing with the dog at the pen?

Chapters 9 and 10
1. What is the first question that Marty's mother asks him about the dog?
2. Why won't Marty's mother agree to keep the dog's presence a secret from Marty's father?
3. Why does Marty think that Shiloh is really more his than Judd's?
4. What is the deal that Marty's mother makes with Marty about the dog?
5. Why does Marty decide not to give Shiloh away to a stranger?
6. What do Marty and his father find when they visit Shiloh's pen?
7. What is Marty's father's first question when he and Marty arrive and find the hurt dog?
8. What does Marty's father do with the hurt dog?
9. When does Marty start "practicing the truth" the night that Shiloh gets hurt?
10. What is the second hardest thing that Marty had to do that night?

Chapters 11 and 12
1. What do Marty's parents argue about the night that Shiloh is hurt?
2. What discovery does David make up on the hill and how does the discovery and its aftermath emphasize Marty and David's friendship?
3. Why does Doc Murphy bring the dog to Marty that afternoon?
4. What firm decision does Marty make once he has Shiloh in his house?
5. Why does Marty's father make Marty tell Judd the story of how Shiloh got to be in the Preston home?
6. What does Judd say when he sees what shape Shiloh is in?
7. What question does Marty's mother ask Judd when he visits and how does Judd respond?

Shiloh Short Answer Study Questions page 3

Chapters 13, 14, and 15
1. Why does Marty decide to go to see Judd early in the morning?
2. Why does Marty think that his talking with Judd could get his father into a lot of trouble?
3. How does Judd try to justify having shot the deer?
4. Why is Judd so shocked when Marty talks back to him?
5. What does Marty threaten to do to Judd?
6. What suddenly makes Marty think that he is no better than Judd?
7. What does Marty ask Judd to put in writing?
8. Why does Judd say that the written agreement he made isn't worth anything?
9. What makes Marty feel somewhat sympathetic toward Judd?
10. What gift does Judd give Marty at the end of the book?

Key: Short Answer Study Questions - Shiloh

Chapters 1 and 2
1. When does Marty Preston first show that he cares about animals?
   Marty first shows that he cares about animals when he and his family are eating a rabbit dinner and Marty worries about how the animal died.

2. When is Marty's favorite time to go up into the hills?
   Marty likes to go up into the hills very early in the morning.

3. What does Marty find up in the hills in the first chapter?
   Marty finds a young beagle dog.

4. What is Marty's reaction when he sees the beagle dog cringe?
   Marty's reaction is that somebody has been kicking, maybe even beating, the dog.

5. Why won't Marty's mother let Marty have a dog?
   Marty's mother won't let him have a dog because the family can't afford to feed a dog and take it to the vet when it is sick.

6. Why does Marty name the dog "Shiloh"?
   Marty names the dog "Shiloh" because he found it up in Shiloh, across the bridge.

7. How old are Marty's sisters and what are their names?
   Marty's sisters are Becky and Dara Lynn. Becky is three; Dara Lynn is seven.

8. What does Marty's father say they have to do with the dog?
   Marty's father says they have to return the dog to its probable owner.

9. How does Marty's father respond to Marty's complaints about how Judd Travers treats his dogs?
   Marty's father reacts by saying that many animals are mistreated in the area and that it is the owner who gets to decide how an animal is treated.

10. What does Judd do to the dog that convinces Marty that he was right to mistrust Judd?
    Judd kicks the dog and then says he'll beat him if he wanders off again.

Chapters 3 and 4
1. By the morning after finding the dog, what has Marty decided to do?
   By morning Marty has decided that he will have to buy Shiloh from Judd.

Shiloh Key: Short Answer Study Questions page 2

2. Why isn't Marty paid for babysitting his two younger sisters?
   Marty isn't paid for babysitting because his father says that everyone who lives in the house has to share in the family's responsibilities.

3. What does Marty think about when he sees his sisters catching lightning bugs and putting them in a jar?
   When he sees his sisters catching lightning bugs and putting them in a jar, Marty thinks of Shiloh all chained up at Judd's place.

4. Why does Judd say he keeps his dogs lean and mean?
   Judd says he keeps his dogs lean and mean so they will hunt better.

5. What does Judd tell Marty about naming dogs?
   Judd says that he never names any of his dogs.

6. What dead animal does Marty remember finding up on the ridge?
   Marty remembers finding a dead dog up on the ridge.

7. What special financial responsibility do Marty's parents have?
   Marty's parents have to help to pay for nursing care for his paternal grandmother.

8. What is the first promise that Marty breaks?
   The first promise that Marty breaks is that he doesn't return Shiloh to Judd Travers when he sees the dog loose again.

9. What promise does Marty make to Shiloh?
   Marty promises Shiloh that Judd Travers will never kick him again.

10. What does Marty build for Shiloh?
    Marty builds a pen for Shiloh.

Chapters 5 and 6
1. What three problems does Marty have to solve in this section?
   Marty has to figure out where to keep Shiloh hidden, how to assure that the dog will keep quiet, and how to get enough food out of the house to feed the dog twice a day.

Shiloh Key : Short Answer Study Questions page 3

2. What system does Marty create for saving some of his dinner for Shiloh?
   Marty says he is too hungry to eat all of his dinner and wants to save some of it for later. Then he puts it in the refrigerator and takes it to the dog later that evening.

3. What lie does Marty tell his parents in order to get out of the house to see Shiloh?
   Marty tells his parents that he is going up on a far hill to practice shoot with his .22.

4. Why does Judd visit the Preston family just as Marty returns home?
   Judd is visiting the Preston family to find out if they have seen his dog.

5. What other dog does Marty tell Judd he has seen?
   Marty tells Judd that he has seen Bakers' German Shepherd.

6. How does Marty rationalize his second lie to Judd Travers?
   Marty rationalizes his second lie by thinking that he hasn't told an outright lie but has only just kept some information from Judd.

7. What question does Marty pose to Jesus?
   Marty asks if Jesus wants him to be one hundred percent honest and return Shiloh to Judd to be beaten or keep Shiloh and fatten him up to glorify creation.

8. Why doesn't Marty want David Howard to visit him?
   Marty doesn't want David to visit him because having David around would make it much harder to conceal Shiloh.

9. What does Marty start to learn abut lying when he tells his parents that there isn't much for David to do on a visit to the Preston house?
   Marty starts to learn that one lie leads to another and, before you know it, your whole life can be a lie.

10. How old is Marty?
    Marty is eleven.

<u>Chapters 7 and 8</u>
1. What kind of pet does David have and what is its name?
   David has a hermit crab named "Hermie."

Shiloh Key: Short Answer Study Questions page 4

2. When Marty lets Mrs. Howard pack him a second "lunch" to take home with him, what does Marty start to think about lying.
   Marty starts to think that a lie doesn't seem like a lie anymore when it's meant to save a dog and that right and wrong are all mixed up in his head.

3. Why does Mr. Wallace at the corner store sell Marty some old food at a cheap price?
   Mr. Wallace assumes that the Preston family is in financial difficulty and needs the food for their supper.

4. How does Marty justify the lies he keeps telling to people?
   Marty justifies the lies by thinking that if he went to heaven and looked down to see Shiloh left alone behind, he (Marty) would run away from heaven for sure.

5. Why do people on Marty's father's postal route start leaving him more food?
   The people think that the Preston family is in financial difficulty and needs the food.

6. When does Marty get his first real chance to play with Shiloh and bring the dog into the house?
   Marty gets this chance when everyone in the family but him goes into town.

7. Why is Marty's mother worried about frown lines?
   Marty's mother says that she must be doing a lot of frowning because people in town asked her how she was feeling and one wanted to know what she took for headaches.

8. Who finally discovers Marty playing with the dog at the pen?
   His mother finds Marty playing with the dog at the pen.

Chapters 9 and 10
1. What is the first question that Marty's mother asks him about the dog?
   Marty's mother asks how long Marty has had the dog up on the hill.

2. Why won't Marty's mother agree to keep the dog's presence a secret from Marty's father?
   She won't agree to keep a secret from Marty's father because he could find out about the dog and would know that she knew but didn't tell him. Then he would wonder how many other secrets she was keeping from him.

Shiloh Key: Short Answer Study Questions page 5

3. Why does Marty think that Shiloh is really more his than Judd's?
   Marty's thinks that Shiloh is more his than Judd's because Judd only paid money for the dog while Marty loves him.

4. What is the deal that Marty's mother makes with Marty about the dog?
   Marty's mother agrees to keep the dog a secret for one night if Marty will promise not to run away.

5. Why does Marty decide not to give Shiloh away to a stranger?
   Marty decides that a stranger might treat Shiloh worse than Judd Travers did.

6. What do Marty and his father find when they visit Shiloh's pen?
   Marty and his father find Shiloh, who has been viciously attacked in his pen by Bakers' German Shepherd.

7. What is Marty's father's first question when he and Marty arrive and find the hurt dog?
   Marty's father's first question is whether or not the dog is Judd Travers' beagle.

8. What does Marty's father do with the hurt dog?
   Marty's father takes the hurt dog to Doc Murphy, the town physician, to be treated for his wounds.

9. When does Marty start "practicing the truth" the night that Shiloh gets hurt?
   Marty starts "practicing the truth" when he admits to Doc Murphy that Shiloh is Judd Travers' dog.

10. What is the second hardest thing that Marty had to do that night?
    The second hardest thing for Marty was to get back into the Jeep with his father.

Chapters 11 and 12
1. What do Marty's parents argue about the night that Shiloh is hurt?
   They argue about Marty's mother's having kept the secret of the dog from Marty's father.

2. What discovery does David make up on the hill and how does the discovery and its aftermath emphasize Marty and David's friendship?
   David finds Shiloh's pen with all the blood still on the ground and then helps Marty to clean up the whole scene.

3. Why does Doc Murphy bring the dog to Marty that afternoon?
Doc Murphy brings the dog to Marty because it was recovering faster than he had expected and because he didn't want his patients to see the dog.

4. What firm decision does Marty make once he has Shiloh in his house?
Marty decides that he can't and won't give Shiloh up.

5. Why does Marty's father make Marty tell Judd the story of how Shiloh got to be in the Preston home?
Marty's father makes Marty tell the story because he believes that it is Marty's story to tell and that Marty should face up to what he has done.

6. What does Judd say when he sees what shape Shiloh is in?
Judd says, "Look what you done to my *dog*!"

7. What question does Marty's mother ask Judd when he visits and how does Judd respond?
Marty's mother asks Judd how much money he wants for the dog, and Judd says that the dog is not for sale.

Chapters 13, 14, and 15
1. Why does Marty decide to go to see Judd early in the morning?
Marty decides to go to see Judd to tell him that he's not going to give Shiloh back, that he wants to buy the dog, and that, if Judd won't sell, Marty will turn him in to the court and tell the judge how Judd treats his animals.

2. Why does Marty think that his talking with Judd could get his father into a lot of trouble?
Marty thinks that he could get his father into a lot of trouble because it is serious business in that part of the country to quarrel with neighbors and have to go as far as the law.

3. How does Judd try to justify having shot the deer?
Judd says that the deer was eating in his garden and he chased after her.

4. Why is Judd so shocked when Marty talks back to him?
Judd is shocked because, in their area of the country, children don't talk back to grown folks.

Shiloh Key: Short Answer Study Questions page 7

5. What does Marty threaten to do to Judd?
   Marty threatens to report Judd to the game warden.

6. What suddenly makes Marty think that he is no better than Judd?
   Marty suddenly realizes that he too is willing to look the other way to get something he wants.

7. What does Marty ask Judd to put in writing?
   Marty asks Judd to put in writing that after Marty works for Judd for twenty hours, Shiloh will belong to Marty.

8. Why does Judd say that the written agreement he made isn't worth anything?
   Judd says that the agreement isn't worth anything because it wasn't witnessed by anyone.

9. What makes Marty feel somewhat sympathetic toward Judd?
   The only nice thing about his father that Judd can remember is that his father took him hunting once or twice. Marty, on the other hand, has done many things with his own father.

10. What gift does Judd give Marty at the end of the book?
    Judd gives Marty an old dog collar for Shiloh.

Multiple Choice Quizzes - Shiloh

<u>Chapters 1 and 2</u>

1. When does Marty Preston first show that he cares about animals?
   a. when he reads a story about animals to his sister, Becky
   b. when he shows concern about how the rabbit that his family is eating died
   c. when he talks about seeing a kitten born in the woods
   d. when he tells his mother that he saw a television show about cows

2. When is Marty's favorite time to go up into the hills?
   a. just after midnight on Fridays
   b. just after dusk
   c. right before lunch
   d. very early in the morning

3. What does Marty find up in the hills in the first chapter?
   a. a wounded hawk
   b. a young beagle dog
   c. Judd Travers' hunting license
   d. a huge German Shepherd

4. What is Marty's reaction when he sees the beagle dog cringe?
   a. He gets angry and hollers at the dog.
   b. He figures the dog must have been born shy.
   c. He thinks somebody has been kicking, maybe even beating, the dog.
   d. He decides that the dog isn't worth his time.

5. Why won't Marty's mother let Marty have a dog?
   a. because the family can't afford to feed a dog and take it to the vet when it is sick
   b. because she really wants the family to get a cat
   c. because she thinks it will make a mess of her house
   d. because she was once bitten by a dog when she was younger

6. Why does Marty name the dog "Shiloh"?
   a. because that is the name of his favorite cowboy show
   b. because his father once had a dog named "Shiloh"
   c. because nobody else in the town had a dog named "Shiloh"
   d. because he found it up in Shiloh, across the bridge.

7. How old are Marty's sisters and what are their names?
   a. Marty's sisters are Grace, 11, and Elizabeth, 6.
   b. Marty's sisters are Pamela, 3, and Kelly Lynn, 2.
   c. Marty's sisters are Becky, 3, and Dara Lynn, 7.
   d. Marty's sisters are Becca, 14, and Kathy Lynn, 1.

Shiloh Multiple Choice Quizzes page 2

8. What does Marty's father say they have to do with the dog?
   a. return it to its probable owner
   b. take it to the local animal shelter
   c. keep it in their house
   d. take it to Doc Murphy for a checkup

9. How does Marty's father respond to Marty's complaints about how Judd Travers treats his dogs?
   a. He laughs at Marty.
   b. He says that Marty thinks too much.
   c. He says that many animals are mistreated in the area and that it is the owner who gets to decide how an animal is treated.
   d. He decides to file a complaint about Judd himself.

10. What does Judd do to the dog that convinces Marty that he was right to mistrust Judd?
    a. He kicks the dog and then says he'll beat him if he wanders off again.
    b. He hits the dog with a whip.
    c. He spits at him.
    d. He says that the dog should be shot on sight.

Shiloh Multiple Choice Quizzes page 3

Chapters 3 and 4

1. By the morning after finding the dog, what has Marty decided to do?
    a. run away from home
    b. ask his Grandma Preston for a loan to buy the dog
    c. buy Shiloh from Judd Travers
    d. try to steal Shiloh and some other dogs from Judd

2. Why isn't Marty paid for babysitting his two younger sisters?
    a. because by law his parents would have to pay him over $5 per hour
    b. because his parents don't think babysitting is important
    c. because his parents never leave him in charge
    d. because everyone who lives in his house has to share in the family's responsibilities

3. What does Marty think about when he sees his sisters catching lightning bugs and putting them in a jar?
    a. being in prison for killing Judd
    b. Shiloh being all chained up at Judd's place
    c. the German Shepherd eating smaller animals
    d. being closed up in his classroom at school

4. Why does Judd say he keeps his dogs lean and mean?
    a. because then they can run faster
    b. because it amuses him to see them lean and mean
    c. so they will hunt better
    d. so they will hate him

5. What does Judd tell Marty about naming dogs?
    a. He says that they should all get names of famous cowboys.
    b. He says he never names any of his dogs.
    c. He says that it's silly to name dogs that could get killed.
    d. He says that ordinary names are best

6. What dead animal does Marty remember finding up on the ridge?
    a. a cow
    b. a dog
    c. a cat
    d. a deer

Shiloh Multiple Choice Quizzes page 4

7. What special financial responsibility do Marty's parents have?
   a. They are involved in a pyramid scheme to make money.
   b. They have invested all of their spare money in the stock market
   c. They have to help to pay for nursing care for his paternal grandmother.
   d. They are saving large amounts of money to send Marty and his sisters to college.

8. What is the first promise that Marty breaks?
   a. He doesn't return Shiloh to Judd Travers when he sees the dog loose again.
   b. He doesn't attend church regularly.
   c. He doesn't write a letter to Grandma Preston.
   d. He doesn't behave as he told Jesus he would.

9. What promise does Marty make to Shiloh?
   a. that he will brush him every day
   b. that he will remove all of the ticks when they get home
   c. that Judd Travers will never kick him again
   d. that he will take him to obedience school

10. What does Marty build for Shiloh?
    a. a big dog house
    b. a special sliding board for dogs
    c. a special kennel for him to sleep in indoors
    d. a pen

Shiloh Multiple Choice Quizzes page 5

Chapters 5 and 6
1. What three problems does Marty have to solve in this chapter?
   a. how to get better grades, how to get along better with his sisters, and how to get a job after school each day
   b. how to beat Judd at cards, how to spit, and how to find more bottles
   c. where to keep Shiloh hidden, how to assure that the dog will keep quiet, and how to get enough food out of the house to feed the dog twice a day
   d. how to spit, how to feed a dog, and how to camp out

2. What system does Marty create for saving some of his dinner for Shiloh?
   a. He says that he is too hungry to eat everything and then saves some food on a saucer for later.
   b. He says that he hates his mother's cooking and then digs leftovers out of the garbage.
   c. He says that he is taking food down to the Howard family.
   d. He says that he needs to save some extra food for his sisters.

3. What lie does Marty tell his parents in order to get out of the house to see Shiloh?
   a. He says that he is going to the movies.
   b. He says that he is going to study with David Howard.
   c. He says that he's going to the library to do research.
   d. He says that he's going up on a far hill to practice shoot with his .22.

4. Why does Judd visit the Preston family just as Marty returns home?
   a. to find out if they have seen his dog
   b. just to be neighborly
   c. to try to get a free meal
   d. to threaten Marty

5. What other dog does Marty tell Judd he has seen?
   a. a wild collie
   b. Bakers' German Shepherd
   c. an Irish Setter
   d. a small Cairn Terrier

6. How does Marty rationalize his second lie to Judd Travers?
   a. He thinks that he hasn't told an outright lie but has only just kept some information from Judd.
   b. He thinks that it doesn't matter if a person lies to someone like Judd.
   c. He thinks that probably God will forgive him because he lied for good reason.
   d. He thinks that Judd is too dumb to recognize a lie anyway.

Shiloh Multiple Choice Quizzes page 6

7. What question does Marty pose to Jesus?
   a. He asks if Jesus wants him to be one hundred percent honest and return Shiloh to Judd to be beaten or keep Shiloh and fatten him up to glorify creation.
   b. He asks Jesus if dogs get to go to heaven.
   c. He asks if Jesus likes dogs.
   d. He asks Jesus which is better, dogs or cats?

8. Why doesn't Marty want David Howard to visit him?
   a. because David is so boring
   b. because he is jealous of all the money David's family has
   c. because having David around would make it much harder to conceal Shiloh
   d. because David is allergic to dogs

9. What does Marty start to learn about lying when he tells his parents that there isn't much for David to do on a visit to the Preston house?
   a. that it's easier to lie than to tell the truth
   b. that one lie leads to another and before you know it, your whole life can be a lie
   c. that some lies are really easy to tell
   d. that some people will believe just about anything

10. How old is Marty?
    a. fourteen
    b. nine
    c. sixteen
    d. eleven

Shiloh Multiple Choice Quizzes page 7

Chapters 7 and 8

1. What kind of pet does David have and what is its name?
   a. a frog named Tony
   b. a dog named Ernie
   c. a hermit crab named Hermie
   d. a fish named Wanda

2. When Marty lets Mrs. Howard pack him a second "lunch" to take home with him, what does Marty start to think about lying?
   a. that it is cool because he gets lots of food by lying
   b. that a lie doesn't seem like a lie anymore when it's meant to save a dog and that right and wrong are all mixed up in his head.
   c. that it's not such a big deal
   d. that he hopes he doesn't get caught

3. Why does Mr. Wallace at the corner store sell Marty some old food at a cheap price?
   a. because he's trying to clear out his inventory
   b. because he really likes children
   c. because he thinks Marty won't notice how old the food is
   d. because he assumes that the Preston family is in financial difficulty and needs the food for their supper

4. How does Marty justify the lies he keeps telling to people?
   a. He thinks that if he went to heaven and looked down to see Shiloh left alone behind, he (Marty) would run away from heaven for sure.
   b. He figures that nobody really cares.
   c. He decides that God has too much to do to catch people up in lies.
   d. He figures that God probably doesn't care much about lying.

5. Why do people on Marty's father's postal route start leaving him more food?
   a. because he has been losing weight lately
   b. because they think he is a really great postal carrier
   c. because they always cook too much food for themselves
   d. because they think that the Preston family is in financial difficulty and needs the food

6. When does Marty get his first real chance to play with Shiloh and bring the dog into the house?
   a. when his mother gets sick and doesn't notice what he is doing
   b. when everyone in the family but him goes into town
   c. when everyone else is asleep
   d. after his father has gone to work and his mother is cleaning

Shiloh Multiple Choice Quizzes page 8

7. Why is Marty's mother worried about frown lines?
   a. because she has recently turned forty
   b. because she looks old compared to Marty's father
   c. because she is very vain
   d. because people in town asked her how she was feeling and one wanted to know what she took for headaches

8. Who finally discovers Marty playing with the dog at the pen?
   a. Doc Murphy
   b. Judd Travers
   c. his mother
   d. his father

Shiloh Multiple Choice Quizzes page 9

Chapters 9 and 10

1. What is the first question that Marty's mother asks him about the dog?
    a. how long Marty has had the dog up on the hill
    b. what kind of dog it is
    c. how old the dog is
    d. whether Marty likes the dog or not

2. Why won't Marty's mother agree to keep the dog's presence a secret from Marty's father?
    a. Then Marty's father would yell at her
    b. She secretly wants to get rid of the dog
    c. He could find out about the dog and would know that she knew but didn't tell him. Then he would wonder how many other secrets she was keeping from him.
    d. She is so terrible at keeping secrets.

3. Why does Marty think that Shiloh is really more his than Judd's?
    a. because he is a much nicer person than Judd is
    b. because Judd only paid money for the dog while Marty loves him
    c. because Marty prays to Jesus while Judd does not
    d. because Shiloh prefers Marty to Judd

4. What is the deal that Marty's mother makes with Marty about the dog?
    a. that she will talk with his father about the dog in the morning
    b. that she will sneak up to Judd's place and try to reason with him
    c. that she will keep the dog a secret for one night if Marty will promise not to run away
    d. that she will let Marty keep the dog if she can get a pet cat for herself

5. Why does Marty decide not to give Shiloh away to a stranger?
    a. because he loves him too much to give him up
    b. because Shiloh is so shy around strangers
    c. because he simply doesn't know any strangers
    d. because a stranger might treat Shiloh worse than Judd Travers did

6. What do Marty and his father find when they visit Shiloh's pen?
    a. Shiloh, who has been viciously attacked in his pen by Bakers' German Shepherd
    b. Shiloh, fighting with a rabid raccoon
    c. Shiloh, waiting to play even though it is nighttime
    d. Marty's mother playing with Shiloh

Shiloh Multiple Choice Quizzes page 10

7. What is Marty's father's first question when he and Marty arrive and find the hurt dog?
   a. what kind of dog it is
   b. how old the dog is
   c. whether or not the dog has bitten anyone
   d. whether or not the dog is Judd Travers' beagle

8. What does Marty's father do with the hurt dog?
   a. takes him to Doc Murphy, the town physician, to be treated for his wounds
   b. takes him to the local animal shelter and turns him in
   c. takes him home and treats him himself
   d. returns him to Judd Travers

9. When does Marty start "practicing the truth" the night that Shiloh gets hurt?
   a. when his father catches him with the dog
   b. when his mother says that he must tell his father the truth
   c. when he admits to Doc Murphy that Shiloh is Judd Travers' dog
   d. when Shiloh appears to be dead

10. What is the second hardest thing that Marty had to do that night?
    a. eat his mother's squash
    b. shoot Bakers' German Shepherd
    c. get back into the Jeep with his father
    d. tell his sisters about the dog

Shiloh Multiple Choice Quizzes page 11

Chapters 11 and 12

1. What do Marty's parents argue about the night that Shiloh is hurt?
   a. money
   b. Grandma Preston
   c. whether dogs are better than cats
   d. Marty's mother's having kept the secret of the dog from Marty's father

2. What discovery does David make up on the hill and how does the discovery and its aftermath emphasize Marty and David's friendship?
   a. David finds his kite that Marty stole from him, but he forgives Marty for doing it.
   b. David finds the bloody pen but then helps Marty to clean up the whole scene.
   c. David finds the dead dog but then promises to keep it a secret.
   d. David finds a dead deer, but he agrees to help Marty to steal the carcass.

3. Why does Doc Murphy bring the dog to Marty that afternoon?
   a. because it was recovering faster than he had expected and because he didn't want his patients to see the dog
   b. because he knew Marty didn't have much money and having Shiloh at the doctor's office was expensive
   c. because he had to drive down near Marty's house anyway
   d. because he really didn't want a sick dog in his office

4. What firm decision does Marty make once he has Shiloh in his house?
   a. that he doesn't really like the dog so much really
   b. that he can't and won't give Shiloh up
   c. that the name Shiloh doesn't really fit the dog's personality
   d. that he really had a criminal mentality

5. Why does Marty's father make Marty tell Judd the story of how Shiloh got to be in the Preston home?
   a. because he feels that Marty needs to be punished
   b. because he believes that it is Marty's story to tell and that Marty should face up to what he has done
   c. because he believes in tough love
   d. because he himself doesn't remember how the dog got there

6. What does Judd say when he sees the shape Shiloh is in?
   a. "Look what you done to my dog!"
   b. "Dang, now the dog ain't worth a nickel."
   c. "Well, what the heck, you can keep him now."
   d. "You are going to prison, Marty."

Shiloh Multiple Choice Quizzes page 12

7. What question does Marty's mother ask Judd when he visits and how does Judd respond?
    a. She asks Judd if he likes dogs, and Judd says he does.
    b. She asks Judd if he understands the fines for pet abuse.
    c. She asks Judd how much money he wants for the dog, and Judd says that the dog is not for sale.
    d. She asks Judd if he has ever had a dog he loved, and Judd says no.

Shiloh Multiple Choice Quizzes page 13

<u>Chapters 13, 14, and 15</u>
1. Why does Marty decide to go to see Judd early in the morning?
    a. because he hopes to be able to kill Judd when he first gets up
    b. because Judd is always pretty dumb early in the morning
    c. because Marty himself thinks best early in the morning
    d. because he wants to tell Judd that he's not going to give Shiloh back, that he wants to buy the dog, and that, if Judd won't sell, Marty will turn him in to the court and tell the judge how Judd treats his animals

2. Why does Marty think that his talking with Judd could get his father into a lot of trouble?
    a. because West Virginia has laws about children talking to people named Judd
    b. because Judd will probably come looking for a fight with Marty's father
    c. because it is serious business in that part of the country to quarrel with neighbors and have to go as far as the law
    d. because Judd is sure to sue Marty's father

3. How does Judd try to justify having shot the deer?
    a. He says that the deer was eating in his garden and he chased after her.
    b. He said that he didn't know his gun was loaded.
    c. He says that he wasn't even aiming for the deer.
    d. He says that the deer actually dropped dead.

4. Why is Judd so shocked when Marty talks back to him?
    a. because he always thought Marty and his father were weaklings
    b. because Marty knows that Judd could kill him
    c. because, in their area of the country, children's don't talk back to grown folks
    d. because talking back is just not like Marty

5. What does Marty threaten to do to Judd?
    a. Marty threatens to kill Judd.
    b. Marty threatens to pray to Jesus to get Judd punished.
    c. Marty threatens to report Judd to the game warden.
    d. Marty threatens to tell his school teacher about Judd's animal abuse.

6. What suddenly makes Marty think that he is no better than Judd?
    a. He too is willing to look the other way to get something he wants.
    b. They both are cruel people.
    c. Both of them have killed living creatures.
    d. They are both terrible liars.

Shiloh Multiple Choice Quizzes page 14

7. What does Marty ask Judd to put in writing?
   a. a confession that he killed the deer
   b. a proposal for how to raise dogs
   c. that after Marty works for Judd for twenty hours, Shiloh will belong to Marty
   d. that he really is a terrible person

8. Why does Judd say that the written agreement he made isn't worth anything?
   a. because he was drunk when he signed it
   b. because he is illiterate and only signed it with an X
   c. because it wasn't witnessed by anyone
   d. because Marty is too young to make a contract

9. What makes Marty feel somewhat sympathetic toward Judd?
   a. Judd cries when he describes his first dog, a collie.
   b. Judd says that the only thing he can remember is that his father took him hunting once or twice. Marty, on the other hand, has done many things with his own father.
   c. Marty suddenly realizes that his father has lots more money than Judd does.
   d. Judd is bitten by one of his own dogs.

10. What gift does Judd give Marty at the end of the book?
    a. a Bible
    b. an old dog collar for Shiloh
    c. a case of dog food for Shiloh
    d. a new Beagle puppy to replace Shiloh

Answer Key: Multiple Choice Quizzes - Shiloh

Chapters 1 and 2	Chapters 3 and 4	Chapters 5 and 6	Chapters 7 and 8
1. b	1. c	1. c	1. c
2. d	2. d	2. a	2. b
3. b	3. b	3. d	3. d
4. c	4. c	4. a	4. a
5. a	5. b	5. b	5. d
6. d	6. b	6. a	6. b
7. c	7. c	7. a	7. d
8. a	8. a	8. c	8. c
9. c	9. c	9. b	
10. a	10. d	10. d	

Chapters 9 and 10	Chapters 11 and 12	Chapters 13, 14, and 15
1. a	1. d	1. d
2. c	2. b	2. c
3. b	3. a	3. a
4. c	4. b	4. c
5. d	5. b	5. c
6. a	6. a	6. a
7. d	7. c	7. c
8. a		8. c
9. c		9. b
10. c		10. b

PRE-READING VOCABULARY WORKSHEETS AND ANSWER KEY

Vocabulary - Shiloh

<u>Chapters 1 and 2</u>
Part I: Using Prior Knowledge and Contextual Clues
Below are the sentences in which the vocabulary words appear in the text. Read the sentence. Use any clues you can find in the sentence combined with your prior knowledge and write what you think the underlined words mean in the space provided.

1. Ma gives us her <u>scolding</u> look.
   _____

2. Dog goes down on his stomach, <u>groveling</u> about in the grass.
   _____

3. Something really hurts inside you when you see a dog <u>cringe</u> like that.
   _____

4. Once he follows me across the bridge, though, and on past the <u>gristmill</u>, I start to worry.
   _____

5. Shiloh comes <u>loping</u> toward me.
   _____

6. Dad's crossing the bridge by the old <u>abandoned</u> gristmill, turning at the boarded-up school, and for the first time I can feel Shiloh's body begin to shake.
   _____

7. He's <u>trembling</u> all over.
   _____

8. "Yep," he says, <u>thrusting</u> his face in the open window.
   _____

Part II: Determining the Meaning
Match the vocabulary words to their dictionary definitions.

___ 1. scolding   A. shoving
___ 2. groveling   B. reprimanding; nagging
___ 3. cringe   C. place where grain is ground
___ 4. gristmill   D. shaking from fear or excitement
___ 5. loping   E. cringing
___ 6. abandoned   F. deserted; forsaken
___ 7. trembling   G. running easily
___ 8. thrusting   H. shrink, cower

Shiloh Vocabulary page 2   Chapters 3 and 4

Part I: Using Prior Knowledge and Contextual Clues
Below are the sentences in which the vocabulary words appear in the text. Read the sentence. Use any clues you can find in the sentence combined with your prior knowledge and write what you think the underlined words mean in the space provided.

9. Dara Lynn shrugs.
_____

10. Next morning Dad gives me a nudge when he comes through to the kitchen, and I'm up like a shot.
_____

11. Bats her eyelashes against my skin, feels like a moth's wings.
_____

12. But I'm mad, too. "Better than callin' him 'Git' or 'Scram.'"
_____

13. If we'd had enough money for me to have a dog and buy its food and pay the vet and everything, I would have had one by now.
_____

14. It isn't that we're rock-poor; trouble is that Grandma Preston's got real feeble, and she's being cared for by Dad's sister over in Clarksburg.
_____

15. The problem is looking me square in the face.
_____

16. I'm tense as a cricket that night.
_____

Part II: Determining the Meaning - Match the vocabulary words to their dictionary definitions.
___ 9. shrugs   A. gentle push
___ 10. nudge   B. honest; direct
___ 11. bats   C. raises shoulders
___ 12. scram   D. weak
___ 13. vet   E. person who cares medically for animals
___ 14. feeble   F. Get out! Go away!
___ 15. square   G. flutters
___ 16. tense   H. tightly stretched

Shiloh Vocabulary page 3   Chapters 5 and 6

Part I: Using Prior Knowledge and Contextual Clues

Below are the sentences in which the vocabulary words appear in the text. Read the sentence. Use any clues you can find in the sentence combined with your prior knowledge and write what you think the underlined words mean in the space provided.

17. Just out of the woods on the other side of the hill, there's a meadow, and I slump down in the grass to rest.

18. Forks continue clinking on the table….

19. Gradually the kitchen clatter dies down.

20. I stand rooted to the ground at the side of the house.

21. Nothing I'd told Judd was an outright lie, but what I'd kept inside myself made him think that I hadn't seen his dog at all.

22. But the way I figure, if it's food from my own plate I would have eaten myself but don't, what's the harm in that?

23. Just for devilment, she plunks herself down beside me in that swing and starts doin' everything I do.

24. The boldness in my chest is growing, taking up all the air.

Part II: Determining the Meaning - Match the vocabulary words to their dictionary definitions.

___ 17. slump   A. making a light, sharp ringing sound
___ 18. clinking   B. firmly established, set
___ 19. clatter   C. wrong
___ 20. rooted   D. fearlessness and daring
___ 21. outright   E. fall, sink, droop
___ 22. harm   F. mischief, annoyance
___ 23. devilment   G. din, racket, noise
___ 24. boldness   H. complete

Shiloh Vocabulary page 4 Chapters 7 and 8

Part I: Using Prior Knowledge and Contextual Clues

Below are the sentences in which the vocabulary words appear in the text. Read the sentence. Use any clues you can find in the sentence combined with your prior knowledge and write what you think the underlined words mean in the space provided.

25   First time I ever saw any <u>envy</u> in my ma.
_____

26. "My first <u>pet</u>!" David says.
_____

27. He skids along the <u>maze</u>, looking which way to go, and we laugh when he gets himself in a dead end.
_____

28. First I go down the street to the corner store and ask Mr. Wallace does he have any sort of old cheese or lunch meat he can sell me <u>cheap</u>.
_____

29. Next problem I got to solve, though, is how to keep all this stuff from <u>spoiling</u> in the July heat.
_____

30. Thinks maybe he could find himself some <u>quail</u> over there, he says.
_____

31. …and he goes right to the gunnysacks in the lean-to, he's so <u>tuckered</u> out.
_____

32. …Becky and Dara Lynn's turning <u>somersaults</u> in the grass.
_____

Part II: Determining the Meaning

Match the vocabulary words to their dictionary definitions.

___ 25. envy   A. rotting; decaying
___ 26. pet   B. at low cost; inexpensive
___ 27. maze   C. network of interconnecting pathways
___ 28. cheap   D. animal kept for amusement or companionship
___ 29. spoiling   E. resentment caused by desire for another's possessions
___ 30. quail   F. acrobatic stunt in which the body rolls in a circle
___ 31. tuckered   G. small chicken-like game bird
___ 32. somersault   H. tired

Shiloh Vocabulary page 5 Chapters 9 and 10

Part I: Using Prior Knowledge and Contextual Clues
Below are the sentences in which the vocabulary words appear in the text. Read the sentence. Use any clues you can find in the sentence combined with your prior knowledge and write what you think the underlined words mean in the space provided.

33. Not one trace of a smile on her face.
_____

34. "Well, I had my suspicions before, but it was the squash that did it."
_____

35. Then I hear a loud yelp, then a snarl and a growl, and suddenly the air is filled with yelps, and it's the worst kind of noise you can think of.
_____

36. And I'm bent over there in the beam of Dad's flashlight, bawling, and I don't even care.
_____

37. I can see Shiloh wince and pull back on his leg where it hurts.
_____

38. …if you could take a look at him, see if he can be saved, I'd be much obliged.
_____

39. Something to make Shiloh numb, maybe.
_____

40. For once in my eleven years, I think I have my dad stumped.
_____

Part II: Determining the Meaning - Match the vocabulary words to their dictionary definitions.

___ 33. trace   A. puzzled; baffled
___ 34. suspicions   B. sobbing loudly; crying; wailing
___ 35. yelp   C. unable to feel, move, normally
___ 36. bawling   D. hints, feelings of distrust
___ 37. wince   E. obligated; grateful
___ 38. obliged   F. visual mark or sign
___ 39. numb   G. short, sharp bark or cry
___ 40. stumped   H. move involuntarily, as in pain

Shiloh Vocabulary page 6 <u>Chapters 11 and 12</u>

Part I: Using Prior Knowledge and Contextual Clues

Below are the sentences in which the vocabulary words appear in the text. Read the sentence. Use any clues you can find in the sentence combined with your prior knowledge and write what you think the underlined words mean in the space provided.

41. I get <u>lonely</u> sometimes up at our house, but today I want to be with that loneliness.

_____

42. "What do you want to do?" I ask David, trying to dig up the least little bit of <u>enthusiasm</u>.

_____

43. …the groundhog <u>zigzagging</u> this way and that, David yelling like crazy.

_____

44. I go over and <u>yank</u> his arm and make him sit down.

_____

45. But I got him sewn back up and full of <u>antibiotics</u>.

_____

46. Seems like she can't hardly pass his box next to the stove without reaching down to pet him, making low <u>sympathy</u> noises in her throat, way she does when Dara Lynn or Becky or me gets sick.

_____

47. "Old <u>stray</u> cat," he says, and now I've got David lying.

_____

48. Still, hard to prove Shiloh wasn't <u>mistreated</u> *before* he got to Judd's.

_____

Part II: Determining the Meaning - Match the vocabulary words to their dictionary definitions.

___ 41. lonely   A. excitement or interest
___ 42. enthusiasm   B. abused
___ 43. zigzagging   C. pity or sorrow for distress of another
___ 44. yank   D. sad at being alone
___ 45. antibiotics   E. lost; wandering
___ 46. sympathy   F. making a series of sharp turns
___ 47. stray   G. pull with sudden force
___ 48. mistreated   H. substances used to treat infectious disease

Shiloh Vocabulary page 7 Chapters 13, 14, and 15

Part I: Using Prior Knowledge and Contextual Clues

Below are the sentences in which the vocabulary words appear in the text. Read the sentence. Use any clues you can find in the sentence combined with your prior knowledge and write what you think the underlined words mean in the space provided.

49. Do I really suppose they'd send an <u>investigator</u> all the way out from Middlebourne to see about as man said to kick his dogs

50. "It's only Uncle Clyde and Aunt Pat, and she's <u>allergic</u> to dogs...."

51. <u>Rehearsed</u> my lines so often I can say 'em by heart.

52. He <u>slogs</u> over through waist-high weeds to where the doe lays.

53. And if I *might* could tell, but bargain not to, it's something else again: It's <u>blackmail</u>.

54. "Heeeowl!" I go again, out of joy and <u>jubilation</u>, the way they do in church.

55. "Why, that paper's not good for anything but to blow your nose on. Didn't have a <u>witness</u>.

56. I can feel the sweat <u>trickle</u> down my back and I ain't even started yet.

Part II: Determining the Meaning - Match the vocabulary words to their dictionary definitions.
___ 49. investigator   A. flow or drop in a thin stream
___ 50. allergic   B. person who inquires or examines
___ 51. rehearsed   C. someone who signs a document to make it authentic
___ 52. slogs   D. walks in a slow, labored way
___ 53. blackmail   E. a joyful celebration
___ 54. jubilation   F. practiced
___ 55. witness   G. highly sensitive to physically
___ 56. trickle   H. get by threatening, coercing

Key: Vocabulary - Shiloh

Chapters 1 and 2	Chapters 3 and 4	Chapters 5 and 6	Chapters 7 and 8
1. B	9. C	17. E	25. E
2. E	10. A	18. A	26. D
3. H	11. G	19. G	27. C
4. C	12. F	20. B	28. B
5. G	13. E	21. H	29. A
6. F	14. D	22. C	30. G
7. D	15. B	23. F	31. H
8. A	16. H	24. D	32. F

Chapters 9 and 10	Chapters 11 and 12	Chapters 13, 14, and 15
33. F	41. D	49. B
34. D	42. A	50. G
35. G	43. F	51. F
36. B	44. G	52. D
37. H	45. H	53. H
38. E	46. C	54. E
39. C	47. E	55. C
40. A	48. B	56. A

DAILY LESSONS

LESSON ONE

Objectives:
1. To give an overview of the unit on **Shiloh**, to explain the teacher's expectations to the students, and to hand out relevant information that will assist students in their study of **Shiloh**
2. To introduce students to four themes in **Shiloh** trust, family responsibility, community values, and responsibility for pet ownership
3. To set the tone for the study of **Shiloh** through a series of pictures that students will provide for a bulletin board and various postings throughout the classroom. For now the bulletin board should be divided into four sections, each listing one of the four themes above.

The teacher should demonstrate the idea of the bulletin board pictures by bringing one of his or her own for each section. The teacher should explain why each of the chosen pictures is relevant. The pictures can be from magazines, newspapers, commercial advertising, or a personal photo collection. Any pictures brought in from personal collections should be clearly labeled and students should be warned not to bring in any irreplaceable photographs since items sometimes can be lost or misplaced.

Activity #1
Distribute Writing Assignment #1 and discuss the directions in detail. Give students the remainder of this class period to work on this assignment. Collect the papers at the end of the class period.

Activity #2
The teacher should demonstrate the idea of the bulletin board pictures by posting one of his or her own for each section. The teacher should explain why each of the chosen pictures is relevant.

The teacher should remind students are responsible for bringing one picture for each theme to class and that they will be expected to explain to the rest of the class why they chose their particular pictures. The pictures can be from magazines, newspapers, commercial advertising, or a personal photo collection. Any pictures brought in from personal collections should be clearly labeled and students should be warned not to bring in any irreplaceable photographs since items sometimes can be lost or misplaced.

MATERIALS FOR DISTRIBUTION

Study Guides
Students should preview the study guide questions before each reading assignment to get a feeling for what events and ideas are important in that section. After reading the section, the students will (as a class or individually) answer the questions to review the important events and ideas from that section of the book. Students should keep the study guides as study materials for the unit test.

Reading and Writing Assignment Sheet
Either post a completed assignment sheet on a side blackboard or bulletin board and leave it there for students to see each day or duplicate copies for each student to have. In either case, you should advise students to become very familiar with the reading assignments so they know what is expected of them.

Unit Outline
You may find it helpful to distribute copies of the Unit Outline to your students so they can keep track of upcoming lessons and assignments. You may also want to post a copy of the Unit Outline on a bulletin board and cross off each lesson as you complete it.

Extra Activities Center
The Unit Resource portion of this unit contains suggestions for a library of related books and articles in your classroom as well as some exercises that can be completed individually or in small groups. Make an extra activities center in your room where you will keep these materials for students to use. Explain to students that the materials are available for them to use when they finish reading assignments or other class work early.

Books
Each school has its own rules and regulations regarding student use of school books. Advise students of the procedures used at your school.

Notebook or Unit Folder
You may want the students to keep all of their worksheets, notes, and other papers for the unit together in a binder or notebook. During the first class meeting, tell them how you want them to arrange the folder. Make divider pages for vocabulary worksheets, pre-reading study guide questions, review activities, notes, and tests. You may want to give a grade for accuracy in keeping the folder.

WRITING ASSIGNMENT #1
Writing from Personal Experience

PROMPT
Trust, family responsibility, community values, and responsibility for pet ownership are four of the themes you will encounter when you read **Shiloh**. In **Shiloh**, Marty Preston learns a lot of lessons about these themes. He learns that trust can be gained and lost, that a person has a lot of responsibility as a member of a family, that a person needs to respect community values, and that responsible pet ownership takes practice.

Your assignment is to write a personal essay in which you explain a time in your life when one of these themes provided a memorable experience. Perhaps you gained or lost someone's trust, maybe you learned something new about being a responsible family member, perhaps you learned to appreciate some values in the community where you live, or maybe you had occasion to learn what responsible pet ownership really means.

PREWRITING
First choose one of the themes. Then jot down as they occur to you any ideas you have about the theme. Think about times in your life when one of the themes has been an issue. Did you learn something new about trust? Did you learn what it means to be a good member of a family or a community? Did you act outside of the prevailing values of your community? Have you ever had and/or cared for a pet of any kind?

Put down all of your thoughts and then go back and consider them. Choose one incident to write about. Try to pick the one you think is the most important and the easiest to explain to someone else. Organize your thoughts into a story format. From there you should be able to write your personal essay on trust. Make sure that you're not *just* telling a story; your essay should make a clear point about the theme you have chosen.

DRAFTING
Just sit down first and write out your story. Try to make it as interesting and as clear as you can while you write your first draft.

PROMPT
If there is time during the class period, give your story to a classmate to read over. Ask if there are any points at which your classmate is confused. Ask if he or she understands the story. See if your classmate can express it to you in a single sentence. Ask if there are points in the story where you need to improve your grammar, punctuation, and spelling.

PROOFREADING
Now go back and re-read the story. Check to make sure that every single sentence, every single detail, is necessary for your reader to understand your point. Cut out all unnecessary lines. Check for grammar, spelling, and punctuation.

WRITING EVALUATION FORM - Shiloh

Name _____ Date _____ Class _____

Writing Assignment # _____

Circle One For Each Item:

Composition	excellent	good	fair	poor
Style	excellent	good	fair	poor
Grammar	excellent	good	fair	poor (errors noted)
Spelling	excellent	good	fair	poor (errors noted)
Punctuation	excellent	good	fair	poor (errors noted)
Legibility	excellent	good	fair	poor (errors noted)

Strengths

Weaknesses

Comments/Suggestions

LESSON TWO

<u>Objectives</u>
1. To give students opportunity to understand the tone of the book through displaying their pictures reflecting four themes.
2. To develop research skills and to write to inform
3. To begin completion of Writing Assignment #2 and the Nonfiction Assignment.

<u>Activity #1</u>
Have students post on the bulletin board the pictures they have brought in for the four story themes. Have students explain at least one of their pictures as they are posted.

<u>Activity #2</u>
Assign one of the following topics (or topics of your choice). Distribute and discuss Writing Assignment #2 and the Nonfiction Assignment sheet. Topics for Writing Assignment #2 are taken from the responsibility-for-animals theme. Students should fill out the Nonfiction Assignment sheet for at least one of the sources they used and submit it along with their report. If you like, take students to the library for the rest of the period to begin work on their assignments.

<u>Topics</u>
1. Pet licensing laws in your state
2. Animal abuse laws in your state
3.. How to successfully choose a pet
4. What it takes to become a veterinarian
5. Animal shelters in your region of the country
6. Finding the right dog for you
7. Care, feeding, and training a dog from 8 weeks to 2 years
8. Acquiring and keeping exotic animals in this country
9. The American Kennel Club, what it is and what it does
10. Veterinary care for the first year of your dog's life
11. A particular breed of dog (pick one that appeals to you)

WRITING ASSIGNMENT #2
Writing to Inform

PROMPT

You are reading the fictionalized story of a real event that was experienced by the author of **Shiloh**, Phyllis Reynolds Naylor. In this story, Marty Preston has to learn a lot about what it means to be responsible for an animal. In order to develop your understanding of the theme of responsibility for animals, you are going to do some research before you begin reading the book.

PREWRITING

Your teacher may assign a topic or allow you to choose one. You will research your topic in the library. Look for encyclopedias, books, magazine articles, videos, newspapers, and internet sources. You may also choose to interview an expert on the topic of your choice.

Think of questions you have about your topic and write each one on a separate index card. Then read to find answers and write them on the cards. Take notes on interesting and important facts, even if you did not have questions about them. Cite all references: write the title of the book or article, the author, and the page number for each reference.

Arrange your note cards in the order you want to use your paper. Number them, perhaps in the upper right hand corner. Read through them to make sure they make sense in that order. Rearrange as necessary.

DRAFTING

Introduce your topic in the first paragraph. Tell why you chose it and give a preview of what the rest of the paper will be about. Then write several paragraphs about the topic. Each paragraph should have a main idea and supporting details. Your last paragraph should summarize the information in the report.

PROMPT

When you finish the rough draft, ask another student to look at it. You may want to give the student your note cards so he or she can double check for you and see that you have included all the information. After reading, he or she should tell you what he or she liked best about your report, which parts were difficult to understand or needed more information, and ways in which your work could be improved. Reread your report considering your critic's comments and make the corrections you think are necessary.

PROOFREADING/EDITING

Do a final proofreading of your report, double-checking your grammar, spelling, organization, and the clarity of your ideas.

PUBLISHING

Follow your teacher's directions for making a final copy of your report.

NONFICTION ASSIGNMENT SHEET
(To be completed after reading the required nonfiction article)

Name _____ Date _____ Class _____

Title of Nonfiction Read _____

Author _____ Publication Date _____

I. **Factual Summary**: Write a short summary of the piece you read.

II. **Vocabulary**:
    1. Which vocabulary words were difficult?

    2. What did you do to help yourself understand the words?

III. **Interpretation**: What was the main point the author wanted you to get from reading his or her work?

IV. **Criticism**:
    1. Which points of the piece did you agree with or find easy to believe? Why?

    2. Which points did you disagree with or find hard to believe? Why?

V. **Personal Response**:
    1. What do you think about this piece?

    2. How does this piece help you better understand the book **Shiloh**?

LESSON THREE

Objectives
1. To continue doing library research for the nonfiction assignment
2. To continue research and writing to inform

Activity #1
Either take the students to the library or give them time in class to work on their research projects.

Activity #2
While the writing conferences are scheduled for Lesson Three, you may want to begin some conferences during this lesson if some students are ready. Try to set aside a quiet section of the room for the conferences.

LESSON FOUR

Objectives
1. To participate in a writing conference with the teacher
2. To revise Writing Assignment #2 based on the suggestions made during the writing conference

Activity #1
Choose a quiet location in the room and begin to hold the writing conferences.

Activity #2
Students should be working independently on their research projects when they are not conferencing with the teacher.

LESSON FIVE

Objectives
1. To increase student knowledge about the topics presented in **Shiloh**.
2. To check students' non-fiction assignments

Activity

Ask each student to give a brief oral report about the nonfiction work he or she read for the nonfiction assignment. Your criteria for evaluating this report will vary depending on the level of your students. You may wish for students to give a complete report without using notes of any kind, or you may want students to read directly from a written report, or you may want to do something in between. Just make students aware of your criteria in ample time for them to prepare their reports.

Start with one student's report. After that, ask if anyone else in the class has read on a topic related to the first student's report. If no one has, choose another student at random. After each report, be sure to ask if anyone has a report related to the one just completed. That will keep a continuity during the discussion of the reports.

LESSON SIX

Objectives
1. To preview the **Shiloh** unit
2. To pass out books if they were not distributed in LESSON ONE
3. To relate prior knowledge to the new material
4. To become familiar with the vocabulary for Chapters 1 and 2
5. To preview the study questions for Chapters 1 and 2
6. To read Chapters 1 and 2

Activity #1
Ask students to describe a personal experience with a pet of some kind. Ask students to relate what they learned from their experience.

Activity #2
Make sure students now have all materials necessary for the unit, including books if they were not distributed earlier. You might want to review **MATERIALS FOR DISTRIBUTION** for your own use or to share with students.

Activity #3
Spend a few minutes talking about how the original four themes and the particular research them related to the book the students are going to read.

Activity #4
Do a group KWL sheet with the students (form included) on one of the research topics from LESSON TWO. Students should know something about animals and responsibility for animals after completing their research projects and will have information to share. Put this information in the K column (What I Know). Ask students what they want to find out from reading **Shiloh** and record this in the W column (What I Want to Find Out). Keep the sheet and refer back to it after reading the book. Complete the L column (What I Learned) at that time.

Activity #5
Work through the pre-reading vocabulary worksheet for Chapters 1 and 2 with the students. Tell them they will have a sheet like this to complete before reading each section of the book.

Activity #6
Show students how to preview the study questions for Chapters 1 and 2. Encourage students to predict what they think answers might be, to write down their predictions, and to compare these with their answers after reading the chapters.

Activity #7
If time permits, begin reading Chapter 1 aloud to the class. Invite willing students to continue reading aloud until the end of the class period. Tell students to complete the reading of Chapters 1 and 2 before the next class meeting.

KWL - Shiloh

Directions: Before reading, think about what you already know about **Shiloh** and/or Phyllis Reynolds Naylor. Write the information in the K column. Think about what you would like to find out from reading the book. Write your questions in the W column. After you have read the book, use the L column to write the answers to your questions from the W column and anything else you remember from the book.

K WHAT I KNOW	W WHAT I WANT TO FIND OUT	L WHAT I LEARNED

LESSON SEVEN

Objectives
1. To review the main ideas and themes in Chapters 1 and 2
2. To set up the parameters for Project Animal Rescue

Activity #1
Discuss the answers to the Study Guide Questions for Chapters 1 and 2 in detail. Write the answers on the board or overhead projector so students can have the correct answers for study purposes. Encourage students to take notes. If the students have their own books, encourage them to highlight important passages and the answers to the Study Guide Questions.

Activity #2
Introduce Project Animal Rescue to your students (details included).

LESSON EIGHT

Objectives
1. To become familiar with the vocabulary for Chapters 3 and 4
2. To preview the study questions for Chapters 3 and 4
3. To read Chapters 3 and 4
4. If time allows, to discuss briefly the idea of mutual trust using presentation of this issue in **Shiloh** as a starting point.

Activity #1
Write the vocabulary words on the board. Ask students if any of the words are familiar. Encourage students to guess the meanings of the words. Then distribute copies of the pre-reading vocabulary worksheet. Let students work in pairs or small groups to complete the assignment.

Activity #2
Have students read the study questions aloud to the class. Encourage students to predict the answers.

Activity #3
Divide students into small groups and have each group decide on a definition of mutual trust. Have the students form back into a whole class, and, if time allows, ask that they share their group definitions with the class as a whole.

PROJECT ANIMAL RESCUE

Objectives
Project Animal Rescue is a total class project for use in conjunction with the book **Shiloh** by Phyllis Reynolds Naylor. Since one of the main ideas in the book deals with rescuing an animal and taking responsibility for it, this is a good opportunity to acquaint students with the animal rescue efforts in your town. We seldom hear statistics on the large number of people who lose or abandon unwanted pets in our communities. This project is a way to make your students aware of the problem of pet overpopulation and the inadequate means most communities employ to deal with that problem.

If you have an SPCA facility in your community, choose to have students use that as part of their project. Because most "pounds" have euthanasia policies, it might be preferable to try to find a no-kill rescue operation nearby.

THE PROJECT
This project is separate from the rest of the **Shiloh** unit, so you can either use it while you are reading and reviewing the book or as a separate mini-unit after you have completed the unit test for **Shiloh**. Also, having it as a separate project enables you to either eliminate it or to use it, without disturbing the flow of the unit as a whole.

Assignment #1
Your local television station or newspaper should have some reports/articles on animal rescue efforts. Should you live in a community that is less troubled by unwanted pets, you might want to focus on a metropolitan area nearby. Find several reports/articles on animal rescue and show them to your students. Use them as a springboard for a discussion of the problem of unwanted animals.

Assignment #2
As a class, write a letter requesting the director of your local animal shelter to come to your class to discuss the problem of unwanted pets. Send the letter and then make any necessary follow-up phone calls to make arrangements for the visit.

Assignment #3
After students have the information you gather on the problem of unwanted pets, send them to the library to do some research. Each student should be able to read and summarize at least two articles on the topic. Hint: They might want to read about how an animal shelter is run, how the abandoned pets can be adopted, spay/neuter policies for adopted pets, costs of running the shelter, why people abandon animals in the first place, how to protect against losing a pet, obedience training for dogs, police department use of donated dogs for law enforcement, use of animals in medical research, etc.

Project continued page 2

Assignment #4
After students have done their research, have them give oral reports about the articles they have read so that all students are exposed to the wealth of information that has been collectively read.

Assignment #5
Host the person who was invited to class in Assignment #2. This assignment should be done prior to undertaking Assignment #6.

Assignment #6
Divide students into groups of five or six. Explain that their job is to make a list of reasons why people might abandon their pets and to brainstorm ways that those reasons could be eliminated and fewer animals be abandoned.

Students might focus, for example, on spaying and neutering pets as a way to eliminate an overpopulation of dogs and cats that nobody wants. They could look at tattooing or inserting a computer chip in an animal as a way of lessening chances of losing an animal. They might want to examine local laws.

Appropriate class time will need to be spent on this brainstorming. After the brainstorming has been done, have each student focus on one way that he or she can address the issue of abandoned pets. The way that each students chooses should involve some amount of community involvement (letter writing, discussion groups, articles in the newspaper, having speakers talk at all local schools, other educational campaigns, etc.)

Assignment #7
Actually visit an animal shelter with your class. If you have not already had someone visit your class to speak, perhaps you could combine a visit to a shelter with an opportunity to ask questions of someone knowledgeable there.

Assignment #8
Have students follow through on their ideas for ways to eliminate the problem of abandoned pets. If they have chosen letter writing, for example, have them actually write the letters. If they think that an educational program would be useful, have them design the program. You might want to use some class time to allow students to update the rest of the class on what steps they are taking. Sometimes the other students may be able to make suggestions and criticisms that will be helpful in carrying out the project.

Assignment #9
After the project is finished, have a short wrap-up to allow students to discuss the value of the project overall. Try to get students to articulate what they learned from participating in the project. See if they will do anything differently in the future as a result of the knowledge they have gained.

LESSON NINE

Objectives
1. To become familiar with the vocabulary for Chapters 5 and 6
2. To preview the study questions for Chapters 5 and 6
3. To read Chapters 5 and 6
4. To discuss the main ideas in the first six chapters

Activity #1
Ask one student to announce each of the vocabulary words. Then have that student call on willing students who would like to guess what the words mean. Then distribute copies of the pre-reading vocabulary worksheet. Ask students to complete the worksheets at home and return them the next class period.

Activity #2
Have volunteers read the study questions aloud to the class. Encourage students to predict the answers.

Activity #3
Ask students to volunteer what they think the main ideas are in the first six chapters. Have them tell what they think of **Shiloh** so far. See if they are sympathizing with Marty or with other characters and why. Ask students to vote (1) for Marty's right to keep the dog, (2) for Judd's right to have his dog back no matter what, or (3) for some combination of the two that might amount to a compromise. If time allows, you might want to have a discussion about whether it is ever okay to break a law.

LESSON TEN

Objectives
1. To become familiar with the vocabulary for Chapters 7 and 8
2. To preview the study questions for Chapters 7 and 8
3. To read Chapters 7 and 8
4. To discuss lying, whether there are good lies and bad lies, and whether it is ever okay to tell a lie

Activity #1
Write the vocabulary words on the board. Ask students if any of the words are familiar. Encourage students to guess the meanings of the words. Then distribute copies of the pre-reading vocabulary worksheet. Let students work in pairs or small groups to complete the assignment.

Activity #2
Have students read the study questions aloud to the class. Encourage students to predict the answers.

Activity #3
Divide the class into two sides. Side One is supposed to argue that it is never okay to lie. Side Two will try to propose possible reasons for lying that might prove that it is okay to lie for certain reasons. Have each side choose a leader who can moderate his or her side.

LESSON ELEVEN

Objectives
1. To look closely at some of the language used in **Shiloh**
2. To review standard English grammar

Activity

Read over each of the lines listed below and rephrase them in standard English.

1. The day Shiloh come, we're having us a big Sunday dinner.

2. Shiloh leaps onto my lap, but he don't look too happy about it.

3. "What if he don't?"

4. "I had two of 'em in my wallet when I walked in here, and now I only got one. This here man's got the other, and I want my change."

5. "I'm lookin' to find me a snake stick," I say as if to myself.

6. "Hell, boy, you ain't even halfway. Hop in."

LESSON TWELVE

Objectives
1. To become familiar with the vocabulary for Chapters 9 and 10
2. To preview the study questions for Chapters 9 and 10
3. To read Chapters 9 and 10

Activity #1
Divide the students into small groups. Assign each group some of the words for the vocabulary for Chapters 9 and 10. Ask the groups to guess at the words' meanings.

Activity #2
Keep the students in the same small groups. Ask each group to choose two of the study questions and guess at what they think the answers will be.

Activity #3
If time allows, have the students report to the whole class on the results of their vocabulary and study question guessing. Have the other members of the class raise their hands if they feel that the group reporting is making a mistake on vocabulary or on study questions.

LESSON THIRTEEN

Objectives
1. To become familiar with the vocabulary for Chapters 11 and 12
2. To preview the study questions for Chapters 11 and 12
3. To read Chapters 11 and 12
4. To explain the directions for Writing Assignment #3 (Writing to Persuade)
5. If time permits, try to include updates on Project Animal Rescue if you have done the Project as part of this unit

Activity #1
Go around the room calling on students to guess at the meaning of vocabulary words until you run out of words. If a student guesses at a meaning and another student thinks that the guess is wrong, encourage the second student to guess at a new meaning.

Activity #2
Do the same thing with the study questions, going around the room and calling on the remaining students. If a student guesses at an answer and another student thinks that the guess is wrong, encourage the second student to guess at a new answer.

Activity #3
Distribute the third writing assignment materials and let students write during class time.

WRITING ASSIGNMENT #3
Writing to Persuade

PROMPT

Marty Preston convinces himself that it is okay for him to keep Judd Travers' dog because he loves the dog. He believes that Judd has no right to the dog since he has probably abused it. Pretend that Judd brings a legal action against Marty and his family for stealing and keeping his dog. Write a letter to the court explaining one side or the other. Give the judge reason to allow Marty to either keep the dog or to force him to return the dog to Judd.

PREWRITING

Make a list of reasons on both sides of the case. Then circle all arguments in favor of Marty's position and all arguments in favor of Judd's. Decide which side you want to be on and then start to elaborate on the reasons that support your chosen side of the argument.

DRAFTING

Make an introductory statement that clearly tells why you are writing and what you want your letter to accomplish. Then go on to explain why you think that your side is the correct position. Be sure to use all of the reasons that you listed earlier. Be sure to write clearly, to summarize your thoughts at the end of the paper, and to urge the judge to do what you think should be done.

PROMPT

When you finish the rough draft, ask another student to look at it. You may want to give the student your list and notes so that he or she can double check that you have included all relevant reasoning in your paper. After reading, he or she should tell you what he or she thought was most and least convincing in your letter. Re-read your persuasive paper, taking into consideration the comments made by your critic, and make whatever corrections you think are necessary.

PROOFREADING/EDITING

Do a final proofreading of your persuasive paper, double-checking grammar, spelling, organization, and the clarity of your ideas.

FINAL DRAFT

Follow your teacher's guidelines for completing the final draft of your paper.

LESSON FOURTEEN

1. To become familiar with the vocabulary for Chapters 13, 14, and 15
2. To preview the study questions for Chapters 13, 14, and 15
3. To read Chapters 13, 14, and 15
4. To apply statements directly from the text to a better understanding of character, plot, and/or theme

Activity #1
Write the vocabulary words on the board. Ask students if any of the words are familiar. Encourage students to guess the meanings of the words. Then distribute copies of the pre-reading vocabulary worksheet. Let students work in pairs or small groups to complete the assignment.

Activity #2
Have students read the study questions aloud to the class. Encourage students to predict the answers.

Activity #3
Divide the students into small groups. Assign each group to one of the following statements. Ask them to decide how the quote helps to describe the person whose name follows the statement, how it clarifies the plot of the book, and/or how it connects to one of the book's themes.

1. You ask **me** the best place to live, I'd say right where we are, a little four-room house with hills on three sides. (Marty Preston)

2. "*Git* on down here!" he says, and before I can even give the dog one last pat, Shiloh leaps off my lap onto the ground and connects with Judd's right foot. (Judd Travers)

3. I eat about half my supper, then say, "I been getting this sort of full feeling at dinner, Ma, and then I'm hungry again before I go to bed." (Marty)

4. "Marty!" Mrs. Howard says when I ring their doorbell that sounds like church chimes. "We're *so* glad to see you! Come on in!" (Mrs. Howard)

5. He's sort of talking without looking at me, the way folks do when they don't want to embarrass you. (Mr. Wallace)

6. "I never kept a secret from your dad in the fourteen years we've been married." (Marty's mother)

7. I figure Dad will answer for me, but he don't—just turns to me. "Marty?" (Marty's father)

8. I tell David how hurt Shiloh was and how we've got to wait till tonight to see how he is, and then we go in his pen together, and David helps me clean up the blood—pull up all the grass with blood stains on it and throw it over the fence into the woods. (David Howard)

9. "If I ever saw a snake, I'll bet Shiloh would kill it for me," says Dara Lynn. (Dara Lynn)

10. Only bit of sadness left in me is for the deer. (Marty)

LESSON FIFTEEN

Objectives
1. To discuss the main ideas in the book
2. To review the plot of the book
3. To allow students an opportunity to give updates on Project Animal Rescue
4. To be sure that students are prepared for the Unit Tests

Activity #1
Go around the room, asking each student to tell the plot of a chapter of **Shiloh**. When you have run out of chapters, continue with the remaining students by asking them to tell about each of the book's characters in a few sentences.

Activity #2
After all of the chapters and all characters have been covered, ask students to tell casually what they thought of the book. Some possible questions are, Was it believable? Did it turn out the way they expected? Do they think Marty acted the way he should have?

Activity #3
If you did the Project for this unit, give students a last opportunity to give updates on their work and to hand in any written materials that you wish to collect.

Activity #4
See if students have any questions prior to the Unit Tests.

EXTRA WRITING ASSIGNMENT/DISCUSSION QUESTIONS

<u>Interpretative</u>

1. From whose point of view is the book written? How does this affect our position on the disagreement between Marty and Judd?

2. What are the main conflicts in the story? Are they all resolved? If so, how? If not, why not?

3. What kind of a person is Doc Murphy in the story?

4. Tell what the function of Dara Lynn and Becky, Marty's sisters, is in the book.

5. Do you think that Marty would be a good best friend to have?

6. Write a brief character sketch in which you contrast Marty's mother and father. If you had to choose, which would you prefer to have as a parent?

7. At what point in the book does Marty first recognize that he is not telling the truth?

8. What is the significance to the plot of having Marty's mother find out about the dog before Marty's father does?

9. Contrast Marty Preston and David Howard. Be sure to use details to convey your ideas.

10. At what point in the story was Marty in the most danger?

<u>Critical</u>

11. Is the story presented in **Shiloh** believable? Tell why or why not.

12. How did Marty change over the course of the story? Were the changes positive?

13. Were Marty's parents believable? Support your answer with details.

14. How would the story be different if Judd Travers were the narrator?

15. What would have happened at the end of the story if Judd had not honored the agreement he made with Marty?

16. Does the book present an accurate picture of the relationship between a boy and his parents?

17. Could any of the chapters of the book be eliminated without substantially changing the story?

18. Which chapter is the most important to the plot?

19. What was your reaction to the character of Mr. Wallace?

20. Do you think that Judd Travers was a believable character?

Personal Response

21. Did you enjoy reading the book? Tell why or why not.

22. Did **Shiloh** make you want to read something else by Phyllis Reynolds Naylor? Tell why or why not..

23. Did you think that Marty would have to return the dog to Judd or not? Explain your feelings.

24. If you were Marty's parents, how would you have handled the situation with the dog?

25. What was the best part of the book? Explain.

26. If you had the opportunity to have dinner with Phyllis Reynolds Naylor, what would you like to ask her or say to her?

27. If you were Marty Preston, how would you have dealt with the situation with the dog?

28. What issues in your own life did the book make you think about? Explain.

29. Do you know anybody in your real life who is like one of the characters in **Shiloh**? Explain.

30. Is this a book that you would recommend to someone in your school who has not already read it? Explain why or why not.

Extra Writing Assignment/Discussion Questions continued page 3

<u>Discuss the significance of the following quotations</u>.
1. "You shoot its head clean off?" Dara Lynn asks.

2. "And get out of those wet clothes," Ma tells me. "You want to follow your grandma Slater to the grave?"

3. "They'll die if you keep 'em in a jar," I tell her.

4. "Shiloh," I tell him, as though he knows it's his name, "Judd Travers isn't never going to kick you again."

5. "What you figure on shooting this time of evening?" Dad asks.

6. "H-his dog? Here in this yard? Haven't seen any dog of any kind in our yard all day," I say, coming a few steps closer.

7. "Snake I saw up on the hill this mornin'," I tell her. "Must have been four, five feet long, just lookin' for somebody's leg to wrap itself around."

8. When she sees me studying her, she says, "Marty, I got frown lines on my face? Tell me the truth now."

9. She stops stroking Shiloh and turns on me. "I wish you'd told me."

10. Once Dad turns the motor off, though, and I'm all set to get out, he says, "Marty, what else don't I know?"

11. "Ray…told you I just found out about that dog myself…"

12. "Deer ain't in season, that's what," I answer. "there's a two-hundred-dollar fine for killing a doe."

13. "Why that paper's not good for anything but to blow your nose on. Didn't have a witness."

14. "When'd you first get interested in hunting?" I ask him. "Your pa take you out when you was little?"

15. "Here," he says, and it's a dog's collar—an old collar, but better than the one Shiloh's got now. "Might be a little big, but he'll grow into it."

UNIT TESTS

Short Answer Unit Test #1 - Shiloh

I. Matching/Identify

_____ 1. Mr. Wallace   A.   the community physician

_____ 2. Becky   B.   person on Mr. Preston's mail route

_____ 3. Ray Preston   C.   Marty's older sister

_____ 4. Mrs. Ellison   D.   the community grocer

_____ 5. Dara Lynn   E.   Marty's younger sister

_____ 6. Doc Murphy   F.   Marty's best friend

_____ 7. Judd Travers   G.   Marty's father

_____ 8. David Howard   H.   neighbor who owns Shiloh

II. Short Answer

1. Why won't Marty's mother let Marty have a dog?

2. What does Marty think about when he sees his sisters catching lightning bugs and putting them in a jar?

3. What is the first promise that Marty breaks?

4. What does Marty build for Shiloh?

5. How does Marty rationalize his second lie to Judd Travers?

Short Answer Unit Test #1 continued page 2

6. Why doesn't Marty want David Howard to visit him?

7. Why do people on Marty's father's postal route start leaving him more food?

8. What is the deal that Marty's mother makes with Marty about the dog?

9. Why does Marty's father make Marty tell Judd the story of how Shiloh got to be in the Preston home?

10. What makes Marty feel somewhat sympathetic toward Judd?

III. Essay
What lessons can a reader learn from what happens to Marty Preston in **Shiloh**? Include at least two lessons and give specific examples from the book.

Short Answer Unit Test #1 continued page 3

IV. Vocabulary

Listen to the vocabulary word and spell it. After you have spelled all the words, go back and write down the definitions.

1.

2.

3.

4.

5.

6.

7.

8.

9.

10.

Key: Short Answer Unit Test #1 - Shiloh

I. Matching/Identify

__D__ 1. Mr. Wallace   A.   the community physician

__E__ 2. Becky   B.   person on Mr. Preston's mail route

__G__ 3. Ray Preston   C.   Marty's older sister

__B__ 4. Mrs. Ellison   D.   the community grocer

__C__ 5. Dara Lynn   E.   Marty's younger sister

__A__ 6. Doc Murphy   F.   Marty's best friend

__H__ 7. Judd Travers   G.   Marty's father

__F__ 8. David Howard   H.   neighbor who owns Shiloh

II. Short Answer

1. Why won't Marty's mother let Marty have a dog?

   Marty's mother won't let him have a dog because the family can't afford to feed a dog and take it to the vet when it is sick.

2. What does Marty think about when he sees his sisters catching lightning bugs and putting them in a jar?

   When he sees his sisters catching lightning bugs and putting them in a jar, Marty thinks of Shiloh all chained up at Judd's place.

3. What is the first promise that Marty breaks?

   The first promise that Marty breaks is that he doesn't return Shiloh to Judd Travers when he sees the dog loose again.

4. What does Marty build for Shiloh?

   Marty builds a pen for Shiloh.

Key: Short Answer Unit Test #1 continued page 2

5. How does Marty rationalize his second lie to Judd Travers?

   Marty rationalizes his second lie by thinking that he hasn't told an outright lie but has only just kept some information from Judd.

6. Why doesn't Marty want David Howard to visit him?

   Marty doesn't want David to visit him because having David around would make it much harder to conceal Shiloh.

7. Why do people on Marty's father's postal route start leaving him more food?

   The people think that the Preston family is in financial difficulty and needs the food.

8. What is the deal that Marty's mother makes with Marty about the dog?

   Marty's mother agrees to keep the dog a secret for one night if Marty will promise not to run away.

9. Why does Marty's father make Marty tell Judd the story of how Shiloh got to be in the Preston home?

   Marty's father makes Marty tell the story because he believes that it is Marty's story to tell and that Marty should face up to what he has done.

10. What makes Marty feel somewhat sympathetic toward Judd?

    The only nice thing about his father that Judd can remember is that his father took him hunting once or twice. Marty, on the other hand, has done many things with his own father.

III. Essay
   What lessons can a reader learn from what happens to Marty Preston in **Shiloh**? Include at least two lessons and give specific examples from the book.

IV. Vocabulary
   Choose ten of the vocabulary words to read orally for the vocabulary section of this unit test.

Short Answer Unit Test #2 - Shiloh

I. Matching/Identify

_____ 1. Mr. Wallace   A.   Marty's older sister

_____ 2. Becky   B.   the community grocer

_____ 3. Ray Preston   C.   person on Mr. Preston's mail route

_____ 4. Mrs. Ellison   D.   Marty's best friend

_____ 5. Dara Lynn   E.   Marty's younger sister

_____ 6. Doc Murphy   F.   neighbor who owns Shiloh

_____ 7. Judd Travers   G.   Marty's father

_____ 8. David Howard   H.   the community physician

II. Short Answer

1. What does Marty's father say they have to do with the dog?

2. Why isn't Marty paid for babysitting his two younger sisters?

3. What promise does Marty make to Shiloh?

4. What three problems does Marty have to solve in this section?

5. Why is Marty's mother worried about frown lines?

Shiloh Short Answer Unit Test #2 continued page 2

6. Why won't Marty's mother agree to keep the dog's presence a secret from Marty's father?

7. When does Marty start "practicing the truth" the night that Shiloh gets hurt?

8. What discovery does David make up on the hill and how does the discovery and its aftermath emphasize Marty and David's friendship?

9. What suddenly makes Marty think that he is no better than Judd?

10. What gift does Judd give Marty at the end of the book?

III. Quotations: Identify the speaker and explain the significance of these quotes:

1. "You shoot its head clean off?" Dara Lynn asks.

2. "Last night," I tell him, "Bakers' German Shepherd jumped the fence and tore him up. We took Shiloh to Doc Murphy, and Judd don't know."

3. "They'll die if you keep 'em in a jar," I tell her.

4. "Shiloh," I tell him, as though he knows it's his name, "Judd Travers isn't never going to kick you again."

Shiloh Short Answer Unit Test #2 continued page 3

5. "What you figure on shooting this time of evening?" Dad asks.

6. "H-his dog? Here in this yard? Haven't seen any dog of any kind in our yard all day," I say, coming a few steps closer.

7. "Deer ain't in season, that's what," I answer. "There's a two-hundred-dollar fine for killing a doe."

8. When she sees me studying her, she says, "Marty, I got frown lines on my face? Tell me the truth now."

9. "Marty, I've got to. He ever finds out about this dog and knows I knew but didn't tell him, how could he trust me? If I keep this one secret from him, he'll think maybe there are more."

10. "When'd you first get interested in hunting?" I ask him. "Your pa take you out when you was little?"

Shiloh Short Answer Unit Test #2 continued page 4

IV. Vocabulary

Listen to the vocabulary word and spell it. After you have spelled all the words, go back and write down the definitions.

1.

2.

3.

4.

5.

6.

7.

8.

9.

10.

Key: Short Answer Unit Test #1 - Shiloh

I. Matching/Identify

__B__ 1. Mr. Wallace   A.   Marty's older sister

__E__ 2. Becky   B.   the community grocer

__G__ 3. Ray Preston   C.   person on Mr. Preston's mail route

__C__ 4. Mrs. Ellison   D.   Marty's best friend

__A__ 5. Dara Lynn   E.   Marty's younger sister

__H__ 6. Doc Murphy   F.   neighbor who owns Shiloh

__F__ 7. Judd Travers   G.   Marty's father

__D__ 8. David Howard   H.   the community physician

II. Short Answer

1. What does Marty's father say they have to do with the dog?
   Marty's father says they have to return the dog to its probable owner.

2. Why isn't Marty paid for babysitting his two younger sisters?
   Marty isn't paid for babysitting because his father says that everyone who lives in the house has to share in the family's responsibilities.

3. What promise does Marty make to Shiloh?
   Marty promises Shiloh that Judd Travers will never kick him again.

4. What three problems does Marty have to solve in this section?
   Marty has to figure out where to keep Shiloh hidden, how to assure that the dog will keep quiet, and how to get enough food out of the house to feed the dog twice a day.

5. Why is Marty's mother worried about frown lines?
   Marty's mother says that she must be doing a lot of frowning because people in town asked her how she was feeling and one wanted to know what she took for headaches.

6. Why won't Marty's mother agree to keep the dog's presence a secret from Marty's father?
   She won't agree to keep a secret from Marty's father because he could find out about the dog and would know that she knew but didn't tell him. Then he would wonder how many other secrets she was keeping from him.

7. When does Marty start "practicing the truth" the night that Shiloh gets hurt?
   Marty starts "practicing the truth" when he admits to Doc Murphy that Shiloh is Judd Travers' dog.

8. What discovery does David make up on the hill and how does the discovery and its aftermath emphasize Marty and David's friendship?
   David finds Shiloh's pen with all the blood still on the ground and then helps Marty to clean up the whole scene.

9. What suddenly makes Marty think that he is no better than Judd?
   Marty suddenly realizes that he too is willing to look the other way to get something he wants.

10. What gift does Judd give Marty at the end of the book?
    Judd gives Marty an old dog collar for Shiloh.

III. Quotations: Identify the speaker and explain the significance of these quotes:
1. "You shoot its head clean off?" Dara Lynn asks.
2. "Last night," I tell him, "Bakers' German Shepherd jumped the fence and tore him up. We took Shiloh to Doc Murphy, and Judd don't know."
3. "They'll die if you keep 'em in a jar," I tell her.
4. "Shiloh," I tell him, as though he knows it's his name, "Judd Travers isn't never going to kick you again."
5. "What you figure on shooting this time of evening?" Dad asks.
6. "H-his dog? Here in this yard? Haven't seen any dog of any kind in our yard all day," I say, coming a few steps closer.
7. "Deer ain't in season, that's what," I answer. "There's a two-hundred-dollar fine for killing a doe."
8. When she sees me studying her, she says, "Marty, I got frown lines on my face? Tell me the truth now."
9. "Marty, I've got to. He ever finds out about this dog and knows I knew but didn't tell him, how could he trust me? If I keep this one secret from him, he'll think maybe there are more."
10. "When'd you first get interested in hunting?" I ask him. "Your pa take you out when you was little?"

IV. Vocabulary
    Choose ten of the vocabulary words to read orally for the vocabulary section of the test.

Advanced Short Answer Unit Test - Shiloh

I. Matching/Identify

_____ 1. Mr. Wallace   A.   person on Mr. Preston's mail route

_____ 2. Becky   B.   Marty's older sister

_____ 3. Ray Preston   C.   the community physician

_____ 4. Mrs. Ellison   D.   neighbor who owns Shiloh

_____ 5. Dara Lynn   E.   Marty's father

_____ 6. Doc Murphy   F.   the community grocer

_____ 7. Judd Travers   G.   Marty's younger sister

_____ 8. David Howard   H.   Marty's best friend

II. Short Answer

1. Is the story presented in **Shiloh** believable? Tell why or why not.

2. How did Marty change over the course of the story? Were the changes positive?

3. Were Marty's parents believable? Support your answer with details.

4. How would the story be different if Judd Travers were the narrator?

Advanced Short Answer Unit Test continued page 2

5. What would have happened at the end of the story if Judd had not honored the agreement he made with Marty?

6. Does the book present an accurate picture of the relationship between a boy and his parents?

7. Could any of the chapters of the book be eliminated without substantially changing the story?

8. Which chapter is the most important to the plot?

9. What was your reaction to the character of Mr. Wallace?

10. Do you think that Judd Travers was a believable character?

III. Essay

At the beginning of **Shiloh**, Marty Preston has great compassion for animals but a little less so for some people he knows. He especially dislikes Judd Travers. Explain in detail how Marty learns to feel some compassion for Judd as the story develops. One key is that the book is told from Marty's point of view: look at places in the story where Marty makes Judd a little bit more sympathetic a character than he is in the beginning.

Advanced Short Answer Unit Test continued page 4

IV. Vocabulary

Listen to the vocabulary words and write them down. After you have written down all the words, write a paragraph in which you use all the words. The paragraph must in some way relate to **Shiloh**.

1.

2.

3.

4.

5.

6.

7.

8.

9.

10.

Multiple Choice/Matching Unit Test #1
Shiloh

I. Matching/Identify

_____ 1. Mr. Wallace   A.   the community physician

_____ 2. Becky   B.   person on Mr. Preston's mail route

_____ 3. Ray Preston   C.   Marty's older sister

_____ 4. Mrs. Ellison   D.   the community grocer

_____ 5. Dara Lynn   E.   Marty's younger sister

_____ 6. Doc Murphy   F.   Marty's best friend

_____ 7. Judd Travers   G.   Marty's father

_____ 8. David Howard   H.   neighbor who owns Shiloh

II. Multiple Choice

1. Why won't Marty's mother let Marty have a dog?
    a. because the family can't afford to feed a dog and take it to the vet when it is sick
    b. because she really wants the family to get a cat
    c. because she thinks it will make a mess of her house
    d. because she was once bitten by a dog when she was younger

2. What does Marty think about when he sees his sisters catching lightning bugs and putting them in a jar?
    a. being in prison for killing Judd
    b. Shiloh being all chained up at Judd's place
    c. the German Shepherd eating smaller animals
    d. being closed up in his classroom at school

3. What is the first promise that Marty breaks?
    a. He doesn't return Shiloh to Judd Travers when he sees the dog loose again.
    b. He doesn't attend church regularly.
    c. He doesn't write a letter to Grandma Preston.
    d. He doesn't behave as he told Jesus he would.

4. What does Marty build for Shiloh?
   a. a big dog house
   b. a special sliding board for dogs
   c. a special kennel for him to sleep in indoors
   d. a pen

5. How does Marty rationalize his second lie to Judd Travers?
   a. He thinks that he hasn't told an outright lie but has only just kept some information from Judd.
   b. He thinks that it doesn't matter if a person lies to someone like Judd.
   c. He thinks that probably God will forgive him because he lied for good reason.
   d. He thinks that Judd is too dumb to recognize a lie anyway.

6. Why doesn't Marty want David Howard to visit him?
   a. because David is so boring
   b. because he is jealous of all the money David's family has
   c. because having David around would make it much harder to conceal Shiloh
   d. because David is allergic to dogs

7. Why do people on Marty's father's postal route start leaving him more food?
   a. because he has been losing weight lately
   b. because they think he is a really great postal carrier
   c. because they always cook too much food for themselves
   d. because they think that the Preston family is in financial difficulty and needs the food

8. What is the deal that Marty's mother makes with Marty about the dog?
   a. that she will talk with his father about the dog in the morning
   b. that she will sneak up to Judd's place and try to reason with him
   c. that she will keep the dog a secret for one night if Marty will promise not to run away
   d. that she will let Marty keep the dog if she can get a pet cat for herself

9. Why does Marty's father make Marty tell Judd the story of how Shiloh got to be in the Preston home?
   a. because he feels that Marty needs to be punished
   b. because he believes that it is Marty's story to tell and that Marty should face up to what he has done
   c. because he believes in tough love
   d. because he himself doesn't remember how the dog got there

Multiple Choice/Matching Unit Test #1 continued page 3

10. What makes Marty feel somewhat sympathetic toward Judd?
    a. Judd cries when he describes his first dog, a collie.
    b. Judd says that the only thing he can remember is that his father took him hunting once or twice. Marty, on the other hand, has done many things with his own father.
    c. Marty suddenly realizes that his father has lots more money than Judd has.
    d. Judd is bitten by one of his own dogs.

III. Identify the speaker of the following quotations:
A) Dara Lynn   B) Mrs. Preston   C) Mr. Preston   D) Marty

1. "You shoot its head clean off?"

2. "And get out of those wet clothes. You want to follow your Grandma Slater to the grave?"

3. "They'll die if you keep 'em in a jar."

4. "Shiloh," I tell him, as though he knows it's his name, "Judd Travers isn't never going to kick you again."

5. "What you figure on shooting this time of evening?"

6. "H-his dog? Here in this yard? Haven't seen any dog of any kind in our yard all day."

7. "Snake I saw up on the hill this mornin'. Must have been four, five feet long, just lookin' for somebody's leg to wrap itself around."

8. When she sees me studying her, she says, "Marty, I got frown lines on my face? Tell me the truth now."

9. She stops stroking Shiloh and turns on me. "I wish you'd told me."

10. "Marty, what else don't I know?"

IV. Vocabulary (Matching)

1.	allergic	A.	person who inquires or examines
2.	gristmill	B.	someone who signs a document to make it authentic
3.	abandoned	C.	excitement or interest
4.	trembling	D.	pity or sorrow for distress of another
5.	feeble	E.	hints, feeling of distrust
6.	outright	F.	resentment over desire for another's possessions
7.	devilment	G.	tired
8.	boldness	H.	mischief, annoyance
9.	envy	I.	fearlessness and daring
10.	maze	J.	weak
11.	tuckered	K.	place where grain is ground
12.	somersaults	L.	deserted: forsaken
13.	suspicions	M.	shaking from fear or excitement
14.	obliged	N.	complete
15.	enthusiasm	O.	network of interconnecting pathways
16.	antibiotics	P.	acrobatic stunts in which the body rolls in a circle
17.	sympathy	Q.	obligated; grateful
18.	investigator	R.	substances used to treat infectious disease
19.	witness	S.	highly sensitive to physically
20	blackmail	T.	get by threatening, coercing

Multiple Choice/Matching Unit Test #2
Shiloh

I. Matching/Identify

_____ 1. Mr. Wallace   A. Marty's best friend

_____ 2. Becky   B. person on Mr. Preston's mail route

_____ 3. Ray Preston   C. the community grocer

_____ 4. Mrs. Ellison   D. Marty's older sister

_____ 5. Dara Lynn   E. Marty's younger sister

_____ 6. Doc Murphy   F. the community physician

_____ 7. Judd Travers   G. the neighbor who owns Shiloh

_____ 8. David Howard   H. Marty's father

II. Multiple Choice

1. What does Marty's father say they have to do with the dog?
    a. return it to its probable owner
    b. take it to the local animal shelter
    c. keep it in their house
    d. take it to Doc Murphy for a checkup.

2. Why isn't Marty paid for babysitting his two younger sisters?
    a. because by law his parents would have to pay him over $5 per hour
    b. because his parents don't think babysitting is important
    c. because his parents never leave him in charge
    d. because everyone who lives in his house has to share in the family's responsibilities

3. What promise does Marty make to Shiloh?
    a. that he will brush him every day
    b. that he will remove all of the ticks when they get home
    c. that Judd Travers will never kick him again
    d. that he will take him to obedience school

4. What three problems does Marty have to solve in this section?
   a. how to get better grades, how to get along better with his sisters, and how to get a job after school each day
   b. how to beat Judd at cards, how to spit, and how to find more bottles
   c. where to keep Shiloh hidden, how to assure that the dog will keep quiet, and how to get enough food out of the house to feed the dog twice a day
   d. how to spit, how to feed a dog, and how to camp out

5. Why is Marty's mother worried about frown lines?
   a. because she has recently turned forty
   b. because she looks old compared to Marty's father
   c. because she is very vain
   d. because people in town asked her how she was feeling and one wanted to know what she took for headaches

6. Why won't Marty's mother agree to keep the dog's presence a secret from Marty's father?
   a. Then Marty's father would yell at her.
   b. She secretly wants to get rid of the dog.
   c. He could find out about the dog and would know that she knew but didn't tell him. Then he would wonder how many other secrets she was keeping from him.
   d. She is so terrible at keeping secrets.

7. When does Marty start "practicing the truth" the night that Shiloh gets hurt?
   a. when his father catches him with the dog
   b. when his mother says that he must tell his father the truth
   c. when he admits to Doc Murphy that Shiloh is Judd Travers' dog
   d. when Shiloh appears to be dead

8. What discovery does David make up on the hill and how does the discovery and its aftermath emphasize Marty and David's friendship?
   a. David finds his kite that Marty stole from him, but he forgives Marty for doing it.
   b. David finds the bloody pen but then helps Marty to clean up the whole scene.
   c. David finds the dead dog but then promises to keep it a secret.
   d. David finds a dead deer, but he agrees to help Marty to steal the carcass.

9. What suddenly makes Marty think that he is no better than Judd?
   a. He too is willing to look the other way to get something he wants.
   b. They both are cruel people.
   c. Both of them have killed living creatures
   d. They both are terrible liars.

10. What gift does Judd give Marty at the end of the book?
    a. a Bible
    b. an old dog collar for Shiloh
    c. a case of dog food for Shiloh
    d. a new Beagle puppy to replace Shiloh

III. Quotations: Identify the speaker of the following quotations:
    A) Marty   B) Dara Lynn   C) Mr. Preston   D) Mrs. Preston   E) Judd Travers

1. "You shoot its head clean off?"

2. "Last night," I tell him, "Bakers' German Shepherd jumped the fence and tore him up."

3. "Why that paper's not good for anything but to blow your nose on. Didn't have a witness."

4. "Ray…told you I just found out about that dog myself…"

5. "Shiloh," I tell him, as though he knows it's his name, "Judd Travers isn't never going to kick you again."

6. "What you figure on shooting this time of evening?"

7. "H-his dog? Here in this yard? Haven't seen any dog of any kind in our yard all day."

8. "Deer ain't in season, that's what," I answer. "there's a two-hundred-dollar fine for killing a doe."

9. "When'd you first get interested in hunting? Your pa take you out when you was little?"

10. "Here," he says, and it's a dog's collar—an old collar, but better than the one Shiloh's got now. "Might be a little big, but he'll grow into it."

Multiple Choice/Matching Unit Test #2 continued page 4

IV. Vocabulary (Matching)

1.	allergic	A.	weak
2.	gristmill	B.	practiced
3.	abandoned	C.	mischief; annoyance
4.	trembling	D.	pity or sorrow for distress of another
5.	feeble	E.	person who inquires or examines
6.	outright	F.	resentment caused by desiring another's possessions
7.	devilment	G.	excitement or interest
8.	boldness	H.	tired
9.	envy	I.	fearlessness and daring
10.	maze	J.	shaking from fear or excitement
11.	antibiotics	K.	place where grain is ground
12.	somersaults	L.	deserted: forsaken
13.	suspicions	M.	hints; feelings of distrust
14.	obliged	N.	highly sensitive to physically
15.	enthusiasm	O.	network of interconnecting pathways
16.	tuckered	P.	acrobatic stunt in which the body rolls in a circle
17.	sympathy	Q.	get by threatening, coercing
18.	investigator	R.	substances used to treat infectious disease
19.	rehearsed	S.	complete
20	blackmail	T.	obligated; grateful

ANSWER SHEET - *Shiloh*
Multiple Choice Unit Tests

I. Matching
1. ___
2. ___
3. ___
4. ___
5. ___
6. ___
7. ___
8. ___

II. Multiple Choice

1. (A) (B) (C) (D)
2. (A) (B) (C) (D)
3. (A) (B) (C) (D)
4. (A) (B) (C) (D)
5. (A) (B) (C) (D)
6. (A) (B) (C) (D)
7. (A) (B) (C) (D)
8. (A) (B) (C) (D)
9. (A) (B) (C) (D)
10. (A) (B) (C) (D)

III. Quotations

1. ___
2. ___
3. ___
4. ___
5. ___
6. ___
7. ___
8. ___
9. ___
10. ___

IV. Vocabulary
1. ___
2. ___
3. ___
4. ___
5. ___
6. ___
7. ___
8. ___
9. ___
10. ___
11. ___
12. ___
13. ___
14. ___
15. ___
16. ___
17. ___
18. ___
19. ___
20. ___

KEY MULTIPLE CHOICE UNIT TEST 1 - *Shiloh*

I. Matching
1.   D
2.   E
3.   G
4.   B
5.   C
6.   A
7.   H
8.   F

II. Multiple Choice

1. ( ) (B) (C) (D)
2. (A) ( ) (C) (D)
3. ( ) (B) (C) (D)
4. (A) (B) (C) ( )
5. ( ) (B) (C) (D)
6. (A) (B) ( ) (D)
7. (A) (B) (C) ( )
8. (A) (B) ( ) (D)
9. (A) ( ) (C) (D)
10. (A) ( ) (C) (D)

III. Quotations
1.   A
2.   B
3.   D
4.   D
5.   C
6.   A
7.   A
8.   B
9.   B
10. C

IV. Vocabulary
1.   S
2.   K
3.   L
4.   M
5.   J
6.   N
7.   H
8.   I
9.   F
10. O
11. G
12. P
13. E
14. Q
15. C
16. R
17. D
18. A
19. B
20. T

KEY MULTIPLE CHOICE UNIT TEST 2 - *Shiloh*

I. Matching
1. C
2. E
3. H
4. B
5. D
6. F
7. G
8. A

II. Multiple Choice

1. ( ) (B) (C) (D)
2. (A) (B) (C) ( )
3. (A) (B) ( ) (D)
4. (A) (B) ( ) (D)
5. (A) (B) (C) ( )
6. (A) (B) ( ) (D)
7. (A) (B) ( ) (D)
8. (A) ( ) (C) (D)
9. ( ) (B) (C) (D)
10. (A) ( ) (C) (D)

III. Quotations
1. B
2. A
3. E
4. D
5. A
6. C
7. A
8. A
9. A
10. E

IV. Vocabulary
1. N
2. K
3. L
4. J
5. A
6. S
7. C
8. I
9. F
10. O
11. R
12. P
13. M
14. T
15. G
16. H
17. D
18. E
19. B
20. Q

UNIT RESOURCE MATERIALS

Bulletin Board Activities - Shiloh

1. Save a space for students' best writing. Make a nice border. Cut out letters THE BEST or FRIENDS OF SHILOH or PHYLLIS REYNOLDS NAYLOR FAN CLUB with a picture of a dog, possibly a dog and a blue ribbon—whatever title and picture you want to show the meaning of the space. Staple up the best writing samples (or quizzes or whatever you have graded) on colorful paper.

2. Bring in (or have students bring in) pictures from magazines and newspapers of people with their dogs. Make a collage if you have enough different pictures (or post individual pictures on colorful paper if you have only a few pictures). This could also be an extension of your introductory activity. You could have the border and title done for the bulletin board and invite students to staple up their own pictures. It will only take a few minutes of class time, students will enjoy it, and you will get your bulletin board done in a hurry.

3. Have students look in newspapers for either dogs available for adoption from a local shelter, dogs advertised in a Pets for Sale section, or dogs advertised in the Lost and Found section. Ask students to make up a little story about each dog pictured. Try to get them to tell the circumstances of why the dog is available for adoption or for sale or is lost.

4. Let students choose types of dogs that interest them. Then get them to bring in a picture of their chosen breed (mixed breeds are included, of course). Have students research briefly the qualities (roots, physical description, traits, etc.). Then ask students to post the picture of the breed they like and write (or announce orally) some descriptions that are typical of that breed of dog. If they prefer mixed breeds, then they can get credit for listing almost any description and any dog traits. Try to get the students to choose a variety of different breeds.

5. See the introductory activity in Lesson One.

6. Do a bulletin board about foods to feed dogs. Have students cut out pictures of different types of foods and then go to the grocery store to price such foods. Have them post the pictures and the prices on the bulletin board.

7. Have students bring in pictures of families doing things together. Have them post the pictures on the bulletin board and tell the class a brief story about what the family is doing and why.

8. Have students bring in pictures of people doing things together in a community. Have them post the pictures on the bulletin board and tell the class a brief story about what the people in the pictures are doing and why.

Extra Activities - Shiloh

One of the difficulties in teaching a book is that not all students read at the same speed. One student who likes to read may take the book home and finish it in a day or two. Sometimes a few students finish the in-class assignments early. The problem, then, is finding suitable extra activities for students.

One useful thing to do is to keep a little library in the classroom. For this unit on **Shiloh**, you might check out from the school or local library other related books by Phyllis Reynolds Naylor or books and articles on family, friendship, trust, animals, or communities.

Other things you may keep on hand are puzzles. There are some in this unit directly relating to **Shiloh**. Feel free to duplicate them for your students' use.

Some students may like to draw or paint. You might devise a contest or allow some extra-credit grade for students who draw characters or scenes from **Shiloh.** Note, too, that if the students do not want to keep their drawings, you may gather some extra bulletin board materials this way. If you have a contest and you supply the prize (a CD, a copy of another book by Naylor, a copy of a book on a subject similar to that in **Shiloh** for example), you could possibly make the drawing itself a non-refundable entry fee. Make sure you assure students that you will continue to place their name on the board with the drawing. This can assure a student that years into the future his or her drawing will still be in his or her old classroom.

The pages which follow contain games, puzzles, and worksheets. The keys, when appropriate, immediately follow the puzzle or worksheet. There are two main groups of activities: one group for the unit; that is, generally relating to the text of Shiloh, and another group of activities related strictly to the vocabulary words in Shiloh.

Directions for these games, puzzles, and worksheets are self-explanatory. The object here is to provide you with extra materials you may use in any way you choose.

More Activities - Shiloh

1. Have students choose to "be" Marty, one of his parents, or Judd Travers. Ask students to keep a journal daily in which they write about what happens to them—but in the voice and character of one of the characters in the book. Everything they write, even if they want to make comments about class to you, should be done in character.

2. Encourage students to write to a local dog breeder who might be tolerant of getting some questions from students. Encourage them to ask the breeder about the time that goes into breeding dogs, taking care of the parent dogs, feeding and taking care of the puppies, etc. Have them inquire about the breeder's daily routine and reasons for being a breeder in the first place. Ask students to report to the class on any interesting responses they may receive.

3. Encourage students to write one of the scenes in the book from the standpoint of Shiloh. What must the dog be thinking about what the humans are doing. This kind of exercise will make students look at the details of the book differently and perhaps more closely than they did on a first reading.

4. Have students pretend that they are Marty or Dara Lynn. Have the "Marty" students write to Mr. and Mrs. Preston just before Shiloh is hurt by the German Shepherd and confess what he has been doing. Have the "Dara Lynn" students write to Marty to tell him that they have discovered his secret. Dara Lynn may take whatever position the students think she would take. Both Marty and Dara Lynn should remain in the character they are in during the book.

5. Let interested students "teach" a class one day. If the number of interested students is sufficient, you could allow the students to work together, make a clear plan, and actually teach a whole class. Feel free to share your daily lesson plans with the students as they prepare to teach.

6. Ask students each to write a letter to the editor of their local newspaper telling what they have found out about unwanted and abandoned pets. You may want to give them some letters to the editor to use as models. You might consider allowing some extra credit for any student who gets his or her letter published.

7. Make a bulletin board with telephone numbers students can call for advice in case they want additional information about the subjects presented in **Shiloh**. For instance, if students wanted information about animal control representatives, breeders, veterinarians, animal rescue groups for dogs like Greyhounds, etc. Students might want this information for purposes of class or for real life situations concerning animals.

More Activities continued page 2

8. For an interesting departure from discussions of dogs and cats as pets, have interested students research unusual animals that people keep for pets. People have been known to try keeping such animals as squirrels, raccoons, bears, and lions in domestic captivity. Have students research the laws about keeping unusual pets and perhaps find stories of people who have tried to do so.

9. If there is a zoo in your area, students might visit the zoo and report on the kinds and diversity of animals available for observation there. If possible, the students should try to talk with the zoo director or with animal attendants about daily care of the animals.

10. Have students talk with a local lawyer about contracts. They might ask the lawyer what he or she thinks about the contract agreed to by Marty and Judd. Encourage them to ask the lawyer to explain verbal contracts to them. This might be an interesting subject to have students report back to the whole class about.

Unit Word Search - Shiloh

Words are placed backwards, forward, diagonally, up and down. Words listed below are included in the maze. Circle the hidden vocabulary words in the maze.

```
B L O O D U J Y H P R U M
E I Y S E J W D S Y O H W T
A E A E N Y L A Y L E O V R
G S R K V A U M Y M A L A W
L C N D S Q K A J A L I P T
E R N N S M N E E R L H C S
K A O C C H Q L S T E S O M
G M T K I T E N N Y R H N Q
N E S S P V E R K D G O T G
P G E W E P F C M C I W R J
D Q R N R A E E D I C A A M
E L P E X B R I E M E R C X
E X K J F S V S K B T D T X
R A P E C A L L A W L N T B
B S U N D A Y K J T F E N H
```

ALLERGIC	DEER	LAW	PET	SQUASH
BAKER	ELEVEN	LIES	PRESTON	SUNDAY
BEAGLE	FEEBLE	MA	RAY	WALLACE
BECKY	HERMIE	MARTY	SCRAM	WVA
BLOOD	HOWARD	MURPHY	SEARS	YELPS
CONTRACT	JUDD	NAYLOR	SHILOH	
DAVID	KITE	PEN	SNAKES	

Answer Key Unit Word Search - Shiloh

Words are placed backwards, forward, diagonally, up and down. Words listed below are included in the maze. Circle the hidden vocabulary words in the maze.

```
      B L O O D D U J Y H P R U M
      E I Y S E       S Y O H W
      A E A E N     A   L E O V
      G S R     A U   Y M A L A W
      L C       Q K A   A L I P
      E R N   S   N E E R L H C S
        A O     H   L S T E S O
        M T K I T E N   Y R H N
        E S S   V E R K   G O T
      P   E   E P F C M   I W R
      D   R N R A E E D I C A A
      E   P E   B R I E   E R C
      E   K     V S   B   D T
      R A   E C A L L A W L
      B S U N D A Y           E
```

ALLERGIC	DEER	LAW	PET	SQUASH
BAKER	ELEVEN	LIES	PRESTON	SUNDAY
BEAGLE	FEEBLE	MA	RAY	WALLACE
BECKY	HERMIE	MARTY	SCRAM	WVA
BLOOD	HOWARD	MURPHY	SEARS	YELPS
CONTRACT	JUDD	NAYLOR	SHILOH	
DAVID	KITE	PEN	SNAKES	

CROSSWORD *Shiloh*

CROSSWORD CLUES *Shiloh*

ACROSS
1 Store having their catalogues delivered by mail
3 What Marty built for the dog
4 Name of Marty's new dog
5 What Marty and his father heard coming from the dog pen
7 What Judd signed about the dog
10 Food that gave Marty's schemes away
12 Marty's father said, "You've got to go by the ___."
15 Marty's best friend's first name
17 Person who worked hard to earn Shiloh
18 Marty's younger sister
20 Owned the German Shepherd in the book
22 What Grandma Preston is
24 David's last name
25 Shiloh was this kind of a dog
26 What Marty told to keep Shiloh
27 Marty's last name

DOWN
1 What Marty threatened his sister Dara Lynn with
2 Marty's father's first name
3 David's hermit crab is his ___
4 Day on which *Shiloh* begins
6 What Judd called some of his dogs
8 David's Aunt Pat is ___ to dogs
9 The real owner of Shiloh
11 Name for David's hermit crab
13 Grocer's name
14 What Marty called his mother
15 Marty saw Judd shoot this animal
16 Initials of Marty's home state
19 David brought this for Marty to play with
20 What David saw all over the dog pen
21 Author's last name
23 Marty's age

CROSSWORD ANSWER KEY *Shiloh*

			S	E	A	R	S								
	P	E	N		A						S	H	I	L	O	H
	E		A		Y	E	L	P	S		U				
	T		K						C	O	N	T	R	A	C	T
			E		J				R		D		L		
			S	Q	U	A	S	H		A		A		L	A	W
		M		D		E		M		Y		E		A
	D	A	V	I	D		R					R		L
	E				W	M	A	R	T	Y		G		L
B	E	C	K	Y		V		I				I		A
	R		I		B	A	K	E	R			C		C
			T		L									E
			E		O		N		F	E	E	B	L	E
				H	O	W	A	R	D		L
				D		Y			B	E	A	G	L	E
						L	I	E	S		V
						O					E
				P	R	E	S	T	O	N

MATCHING QUIZ/WORKSHEET 1 - Shiloh

___ 1. NAYLOR   A. Marty's younger sister

___ 2. HOWARD   B. Shiloh was this kind of a dog

___ 3. CONTRACT   C. Marty's last name

___ 4. PET   D. David's hermit crab is his ___

___ 5. YELPS   E. David's last name

___ 6. SNAKES   F. Name for David's hermit crab

___ 7. SQUASH   G. Marty's age

___ 8. ELEVEN   H. Marty saw Judd shoot this animal

___ 9. LAW   I. What Grandma Preston is

___ 10. SUNDAY   J. Initials of Marty's home state

___ 11. MURPHY   K. The real owner of Shiloh

___ 12. PRESTON   L. What Marty called his mother

___ 13. MA   M. What Marty threatened his sister Dara Lynn with

___ 14. BEAGLE   N. What Marty and his father heard coming from the dog pen

___ 15. RAY   O. Marty's father's first name

___ 16. ALLERGIC   P. Veterinarian's name: Doc ___

___ 17. JUDD   Q. Food that gave Marty's schemes away

___ 18. KITE   R. David brought this for Marty to play with

___ 19. BECKY   S. David's Aunt Pat is ___ to dogs

___ 20. BLOOD   T. What Judd signed about the dog

___ 21. FEEBLE   U. Marty's father said, 'You've got to go by the ___.'

___ 22. DEER   V. What David saw all over the dog pen

___ 23. LIES   W. What Marty told to keep Shiloh

___ 24. HERMIE   X. Day on which SHILOH begins

___ 25. WVA   Y. Author's last name

KEY: MATCHING QUIZ/WORKSHEET 1 - Shiloh

Y - 1. NAYLOR	A.	Marty's younger sister
E - 2. HOWARD	B.	Shiloh was this kind of a dog
T - 3. CONTRACT	C.	Marty's last name
D - 4. PET	D.	David's hermit crab is his ___
N - 5. YELPS	E.	David's last name
M - 6. SNAKES	F.	Name for David's hermit crab
Q - 7. SQUASH	G.	Marty's age
G - 8. ELEVEN	H.	Marty saw Judd shoot this animal
U - 9. LAW	I.	What Grandma Preston is
X - 10. SUNDAY	J.	Initials of Marty's home state
P - 11. MURPHY	K.	The real owner of Shiloh
C - 12. PRESTON	L.	What Marty called his mother
L - 13. MA	M.	What Marty threatened his sister Dara Lynn with
B - 14. BEAGLE	N.	What Marty and his father heard coming from the dog pen
O - 15. RAY	O.	Marty's father's first name
S - 16. ALLERGIC	P.	Veterinarian's name: Doc ___
K - 17. JUDD	Q.	Food that gave Marty's schemes away
R - 18. KITE	R.	David brought this for Marty to play with
A - 19. BECKY	S.	David's Aunt Pat is ___ to dogs
V - 20. BLOOD	T.	What Judd signed about the dog
I - 21. FEEBLE	U.	Marty's father said, 'You've got to go by the ___.'
H - 22. DEER	V.	What David saw all over the dog pen
W 23. LIES	W.	What Marty told to keep Shiloh
F - 24. HERMIE	X.	Day on which SHILOH begins
J - 25. WVA	Y.	Author's last name

MATCHING QUIZ/WORKSHEET 2 - Shiloh

___ 1. JUDD   A. David's last name

___ 2. ALLERGIC   B. David's hermit crab is his ___

___ 3. SEARS   C. What Judd called some of his dogs

___ 4. MA   D. Author's last name

___ 5. WVA   E. Marty's father said, 'You've got to go by the ___.'

___ 6. BECKY   F. David's Aunt Pat is ___ to dogs

___ 7. SNAKES   G. Store having their catalogues delivered by mail

___ 8. BEAGLE   H. Marty's last name

___ 9. MARTY   I. Person who worked hard to earn Shiloh

___ 10. LAW   J. Owned the German Shepherd in the book

___ 11. SHILOH   K. David brought this for Marty to play with

___ 12. FEEBLE   L. Shiloh was this kind of a dog

___ 13. WALLACE   M. What Marty told to keep Shiloh

___ 14. NAYLOR   N. What Grandma Preston is

___ 15. BAKER   O. Marty's younger sister

___ 16. RAY   P. Marty's father's first name

___ 17. KITE   Q. The real owner of Shiloh

___ 18. ELEVEN   R. Marty's age

___ 19. LIES   S. Grocer's name

___ 20. PET   T. What Marty threatened his sister Dara Lynn with

___ 21. MURPHY   U. Veterinarian's name: Doc ___

___ 22. SUNDAY   V. What Marty called his mother

___ 23. PRESTON   W. Initials of Marty's home state

___ 24. SCRAM   X. Name of Marty's new dog

___ 25. HOWARD   Y. Day on which SHILOH begins

KEY: MATCHING QUIZ/WORKSHEET 2 - Shiloh

Q - 1.	JUDD	A.	David's last name
F - 2.	ALLERGIC	B.	David's hermit crab is his ___
G - 3.	SEARS	C.	What Judd called some of his dogs
V - 4.	MA	D.	Author's last name
W - 5.	WVA	E.	Marty's father said, 'You've got to go by the ___.'
O - 6.	BECKY	F.	David's Aunt Pat is ___ to dogs
T - 7.	SNAKES	G.	Store having their catalogues delivered by mail
L - 8.	BEAGLE	H.	Marty's last name
I - 9.	MARTY	I.	Person who worked hard to earn Shiloh
E - 10.	LAW	J.	Owned the German Shepherd in the book
X - 11.	SHILOH	K.	David brought this for Marty to play with
N - 12.	FEEBLE	L.	Shiloh was this kind of a dog
S - 13.	WALLACE	M.	What Marty told to keep Shiloh
D - 14.	NAYLOR	N.	What Grandma Preston is
J - 15.	BAKER	O.	Marty's younger sister
P - 16.	RAY	P.	Marty's father's first name
K - 17.	KITE	Q.	The real owner of Shiloh
R - 18.	ELEVEN	R.	Marty's age
M - 19.	LIES	S.	Grocer's name
B - 20.	PET	T.	What Marty threatened his sister Dara Lynn with
U - 21.	MURPHY	U.	Veterinarian's name: Doc ___
Y - 22.	SUNDAY	V.	What Marty called his mother
H - 23.	PRESTON	W.	Initials of Marty's home state
C - 24.	SCRAM	X.	Name of Marty's new dog
A - 25.	HOWARD	Y.	Day on which SHILOH begins

Review Game Juggle Letter Clues - Shiloh

ARY	RAY	Marty's father's first name
TPE	PET	David's hermit crab is his ___.
ENP	PEN	What Marty built for the dog
MEEHRI	HERMIE	Name for David's hermit crab
WODRAH	HOWARD	David's last name
RLONAY	NAYLOR	Author's last name
BLEEFE	FEEBLE	What Grandma Preston is
VADDI	DAVID	Marty's best friend's first name
KASSEN	SNAKES	What Marty threatened his sister Dara Lynn with
DOBOL	BLOOD	What David saw all over the dog pen
REBAK	BAKER	Owned the German Shepherd in the book
TROPENS	PRESTON	Marty's last name
CLALEWA	WALLACE	Grocer's name
YUMHRP	MURPHY	Veterinarian's name, Doc ___
VAW	WVA	Initials of Marty's home state
HOHSIL	SHILOH	Name of Marty's new dog
KEYBC	BECKY	Marty's younger sister
DANYUS	SUNDAY	Day on which SHILOH begins
GALLERCI	ALLERGIC	David's Aunt Pat is ___ to dogs.
QSSUHA	SQUASH	The food that gave Marty's schemes away
PLEYS	YELPS	What Marty and his father heard coming from the dog pen
AM	MA	What Marty called his mother
MRACS	SCRAM	What Judd called some of his dogs
GLABEE	BEAGLE	The kind of dog Shiloh is
ROTTNCCA	CONTRACT	What Judd signed about the dog
TIEK	KITE	David brought this to Marty to play with
VEENEL	ELEVEN	Marty's age
DUJD	JUDD	The real owner of Shiloh
AWL	LAW	Marty's father said, "You've got to go by the ___"
RASSE	SEARS	Store having their catalogues delivered by mail
TRAYM	MARTY	Person who worked hard to earn Shiloh
SEIL	LIES	What Marty told to keep Shiloh
REDE	DEER	What Marty saw Judd shoot

VOCABULARY RESOURCES

Vocabulary Word Search - Shiloh

Words are placed backwards, forward, diagonally, up and down. Words listed below are included in the maze. Circle the hidden vocabulary words in the maze.

```
M A Z E M S Q G N I T S U R H T S R S C
M S N G L T W N R N Y Q B O C E T E O M
M V L D I R I I S O W X W O R N U H M Z
Y T W U A A N D T G V I R T I S M E E I
S A R N M Y C L A T T E R E N E P A R G
L P N A K P E O B N E R L D G V E R S Z
O T O K C C F C E E P C E I E E D S A A
G U Q I A E L S C M B H S M N T R E U G
S C U V L N S I L L O E C J B G B D L G
L K A H B I G G I I L A R R N L E F T I
O E I B A R N G N V D P A U N G I C L N
N R L T E R R G K E N V M F I Y Y N S G
E E J L H H M N I D E B Z L Z J E B G S
L D L O P I N G N F S W B B A W L I N G
Y A F E E B L E G B S O Y H T A P M Y S
```

ALLERGIC	DEVILMENT	NUMB	SLUMP	TREMBLING
BATS	ENVY	OBLIGED	SOMERSAULT	TUCKERED
BAWLING	FEEBLE	PET	SPOILING	VET
BLACKMAIL	GROVELING	QUAIL	STRAY	WINCE
BOLDNESS	HARM	REHEARSED	STUMPED	WITNESS
CHEAP	LONELY	ROOTED	SYMPATHY	YANK
CLATTER	LOPING	SCOLDING	TENSE	YELP
CLINKING	MAZE	SCRAM	THRUSTING	ZIGZAGGING
CRINGE	NUDGE	SLOGS	TRACE	

Vocabulary Word Search Answer Key - Shiloh

```
M  A  Z  E     S     G  N  I  T  S  U  R  H  T  S  R  S
      S  N  G  L  T  W  N  R           O  C  E  T  E  O
      V  L  D  I  R  I  I  S  O     W  O  R  N  U  H  M  Z
Y  T     U  A  A  N  D  T     V  I     T  I  S  M  E  E  I
S  A  R  N  M  Y  C  L  A  T  T  E  R  E  N  E  P  A  R  G
L  P  N  A  K  P  E  O  B  N  E  R  L  D  G  V  E  R  S  Z
O  T  O  K  C        C  E  E  P  C  E  I  E  E  D  S  A  A
G  U  Q  I  A  E     S  C  M  B  H  S  M  N  T     E  U  G
S  C     U     L     S  I  L  L  O  E  C     B  G     D  L
L  K  A  H  B  I  G     I  I  L  A  R     N  L  E     T  I
O  E  I     A  R  N     N  V  D  P  A  U     G  I        N
N  R  L     E  R     G  K  E  N     M     I     Y  N     G
E  E     L     M     I  D  E  B     L           E     G
L  D  L  O  P  I  N  G     S     B  B  A  W  L  I  N  G
Y  A  F  E  E  B  L  E  G     S  O  Y  H  T  A  P  M  Y  S
```

ALLERGIC	DEVILMENT	NUMB	SLUMP	TREMBLING
BATS	ENVY	OBLIGED	SOMERSAULT	TUCKERED
BAWLING	FEEBLE	PET	SPOILING	VET
BLACKMAIL	GROVELING	QUAIL	STRAY	WINCE
BOLDNESS	HARM	REHEARSED	STUMPED	WITNESS
CHEAP	LONELY	ROOTED	SYMPATHY	YANK
CLATTER	LOPING	SCOLDING	TENSE	YELP
CLINKING	MAZE	SCRAM	THRUSTING	ZIGZAGGING
CRINGE	NUDGE	SLOGS	TRACE	

VOCABULARY CROSSWORD *Shiloh*

VOCABULARY CROSSWORD CLUES *Shiloh*

ACROSS
1 Person who inquires or examines
7 Resentment caused by desire for another's possessions
9 Reprimanding; nagging
13 Visual mark or sign
14 Short, sharp bark or cry
16 Deserted; forsaken
17 Place where grain is ground
20 Move involuntarily, as in pain
22 Complete
26 Weak
27 Shaking from fear or excitement
31 Fearlessness and daring
32 Puzzled; baffled
33 Lost; wandering
34 Walks in a slow, labored way

DOWN
2 Gentle push
3 Cringing
4 Tired
5 Practiced
6 Running easily
8 Person who gives medical care to animals
9 Rotting; decaying
10 Unable to feel normally
11 Sobbing loudly; crying; wailing
12 Animal kept for amusement or companionship
14 Pull with sudden force
15 Mischief; annoyance
18 Firmly established; set
19 Shoving
20 Someone who signs a document to make it authentic
21 At low cost; inexpensive
23 Wrong
24 Obligated; grateful
25 Din; racket; noise
28 Network of interconnecting pathways
29 Fall; sink; droop
30 Small, chicken-like game bird
31 Flutters

VOCABULARY CROSSWORD ANSWER KEY *Shiloh*

KEY: VOCABULARY WORKSHEET 1 - Shiloh

___ 1. ZIGZAGGING   A. Acrobatic stunt in which the body rolls in a circle

___ 2. SOMERSAULT   B. Making a series of sharp turns

___ 3. ANTIBIOTICS   C. Rotting; decaying

___ 4. SLUMP   D. Obligated; grateful

___ 5. CLINKING   E. Resentment caused by desire for another's possessions

___ 6. FEEBLE   F. Making a light, sharp ringing sound

___ 7. TENSE   G. Wrong

___ 8. ENVY   H. Deserted; forsaken

___ 9. DEVILMENT   I. Person who inquires or examines

___ 10. NUDGE   J. Tightly stretched

___ 11. INVESTIGATOR   K. Firmly established; set

___ 12. OBLIGED   L. Get by threatening

___ 13. SPOILING   M. Place where grain is ground

___ 14. ROOTED   N. Excitement or interest for or in something

___ 15. SLOGS   O. Weak

___ 16. BLACKMAIL   P. Substances used to treat infectious diseases

___ 17. GRISTMILL   Q. Fall; sink; droop

___ 18. OUTRIGHT   R. Running easily

___ 19. ABANDONED   S. Shoving

___ 20. ENTHUSIASM   T. Shaking from fear or excitement

___ 21. SYMPATHY   U. Gentle push

___ 22. HARM   V. Complete

___ 23. THRUSTING   W. Mischief; annoyance

___ 24. TREMBLING   X. Walks in a slow, labored way

___ 25. LOPING   Y. Pity or sorrow for distress of another

KEY: VOCABULARY WORKSHEET 1 - Shiloh

B - 1.	ZIGZAGGING	A.	Acrobatic stunt in which the body rolls in a circle
A - 2.	SOMERSAULT	B.	Making a series of sharp turns
P - 3.	ANTIBIOTICS	C.	Rotting; decaying
Q - 4.	SLUMP	D.	Obligated; grateful
F - 5.	CLINKING	E.	Resentment caused by desire for another's possessions
O - 6.	FEEBLE	F.	Making a light, sharp ringing sound
J - 7.	TENSE	G.	Wrong
E - 8.	ENVY	H.	Deserted; forsaken
W 9.	DEVILMENT	I.	Person who inquires or examines
U -10.	NUDGE	J.	Tightly stretched
I - 11.	INVESTIGATOR	K.	Firmly established; set
D -12.	OBLIGED	L.	Get by threatening
C -13.	SPOILING	M.	Place where grain is ground
K -14.	ROOTED	N.	Excitement or interest for or in something
X -15.	SLOGS	O.	Weak
L -16.	BLACKMAIL	P.	Substances used to treat infectious diseases
M -17.	GRISTMILL	Q.	Fall; sink; droop
V -18.	OUTRIGHT	R.	Running easily
H -19.	ABANDONED	S.	Shoving
N -20.	ENTHUSIASM	T.	Shaking from fear or excitement
Y -21.	SYMPATHY	U.	Gentle push
G -22.	HARM	V.	Complete
S -23.	THRUSTING	W.	Mischief; annoyance
T -24.	TREMBLING	X.	Walks in a slow, labored way
R -25.	LOPING	Y.	Pity or sorrow for distress of another

VOCABULARY WORKSHEET 2 - Shiloh

___ 1. GRISTMILL   A. Highly sensitive to something physically

___ 2. SCOLDING   B. Fearlessness and daring

___ 3. JUBILATION   C. Wrong

___ 4. YELP   D. Sad at being alone

___ 5. ALLERGIC   E. Small, chicken-like game bird

___ 6. PET   F. Abused

___ 7. TENSE   G. Gentle push

___ 8. ENTHUSIASM   H. Lost; wandering

___ 9. STRAY   I. Place where grain is ground

___10. MAZE   J. Short, sharp bark or cry

___11. TRACE   K. Tired

___12. TUCKERED   L. Puzzled; baffled

___13. LONELY   M. Fall; sink; droop

___14. QUAIL   N. Pity or sorrow for distress of another

___15. BOLDNESS   O. Walks in a slow, labored way

___16. NUDGE   P. Complete

___17. MISTREATED   Q. Raises shoulders

___18. HARM   R. Network of interconnecting pathways

___19. SLOGS   S. Cringing

___20. SLUMP   T. Visual mark or sign

___21. STUMPED   U. Animal kept for amusement or companionship

___22. GROVELING   V. Excitement or interest for or in something

___23. OUTRIGHT   W. Tightly stretched

___24. SHRUGS   X. Reprimanding; nagging

___25. SYMPATHY   Y. A joyful celebration

KEY: VOCABULARY WORKSHEET 2 - Shiloh

I - 1.	GRISTMILL	A. Highly sensitive to something physically
X - 2.	SCOLDING	B. Fearlessness and daring
Y - 3.	JUBILATION	C. Wrong
J - 4.	YELP	D. Sad at being alone
A - 5.	ALLERGIC	E. Small, chicken-like game bird
U - 6.	PET	F. Abused
W - 7.	TENSE	G. Gentle push
V - 8.	ENTHUSIASM	H. Lost; wandering
H - 9.	STRAY	I. Place where grain is ground
R -10.	MAZE	J. Short, sharp bark or cry
T -11.	TRACE	K. Tired
K -12.	TUCKERED	L. Puzzled; baffled
D -13.	LONELY	M. Fall; sink; droop
E -14.	QUAIL	N. Pity or sorrow for distress of another
B -15.	BOLDNESS	O. Walks in a slow, labored way
G -16.	NUDGE	P. Complete
F -17.	MISTREATED	Q. Raises shoulders
C -18.	HARM	R. Network of interconnecting pathways
O -19.	SLOGS	S. Cringing
M -20.	SLUMP	T. Visual mark or sign
L -21.	STUMPED	U. Animal kept for amusement or companionship
S -22.	GROVELING	V. Excitement or interest for or in something
P -23.	OUTRIGHT	W. Tightly stretched
Q -24.	SHRUGS	X. Reprimanding; nagging
N -25.	SYMPATHY	Y. A joyful celebration

Vocabulary Juggle Letter Review Game Clues - Shiloh

LDOCINSG	SCOLDING	Reprimanding; nagging
GIEOGRVLN	GROVELING	Cringing
GRIECN	CRINGE	Shrink; cower
RMLIGLTIS	GRISTMILL	Place where grain is ground
NOLGIP	LOPING	Running easily
EBADNANOD	ABANDONED	Deserted; forsaken
GLRMITBEN	TREMBLING	Shaking from fear or excitement
GRINSTTUH	THRUSTING	Shoving
RHSSGU	SHRUGS	Raises shoulders
GENUD	NUDGE	Gentle push
STAB	BATS	Flutters
RMSAC	SCRAM	Get out! Go away!
TEV	VET	Person who gives medical care to animals
BLEEEF	FEEBLE	Weak
QRESAU	SQUARE	Honest; direct
NEETS	TENSE	Tightly stretched
PLSMU	SLUMP	Fall, sink, droop
KNINGLCI	CLINKING	Making a light, sharp ringing sound
TRELACT	CLATTER	Din, racket, noise
DORETO	ROOTED	Firmly established; set
GOTHUTRI	OUTRIGHT	Complete
RHMA	HARM	Wrong
MVEDTINLE	DEVILMENT	Mischief, annoyance
SDNBLOES	BOLDNESS	Fearlessness and daring
YENV	ENVY	Resentment caused by desire for another's possessions
TPE	PET	Animal kept for amusement or companionship
ZEAM	MAZE	Network of interconnecting pathways
PHAEC	CHEAP	At low cost; inexpensive
LPONIGIS	SPOILING	Rotting; decaying
LQIAU	QUAIL	Small chicken-like game bird
KDEUTCER	TUCKERED	Tired
RLEMTSSOAU	SOMERSAULT	Acrobatic stunt in which the body rolls in a circle
CREAT	TRACE	Visual mark or sign

SNOICIPSUS	SUSPICIONS	Hints, feelings of distrust
PEYL	YELP	Short, sharp bark or cry
LIWGNBA	BAWLING	Sobbing loudly; crying; wailing
ENICW	WINCE	Move involuntarily, as in pain
GLOBEID	OBLIGED	Obligated; grateful
BUNM	NUMB	Unable to feel, move, normally
PTEDUSM	STUMPED	Puzzled; baffled
ELLOYN	LONELY	Sad at being alone
MHETSAIUSN	ENTHUSIASM	Excitement or interest
GGGGZZIIAN	ZIGZAGGING	Making a series of sharp turns
NKAY	YANK	Pull with sudden force
IBTCANSITIO	ANTIBIOTICS	Substances used to treat infectious diseases
PYATYSHM	SYMPATHY	Pity or sorrow for distress or another
TYRAS	STRAY	Lost; wandering
DRISMAETTE	MISTREATED	Abused
SRTEIVTIONGA	INVESTIGATOR	Person who inquires or examines
CALLREIG	ALLERGIC	Highly sensitive to something physically
RHADSEREE	REHEARSED	Practiced
LOSSG	SLOGS	Walks in a slow, labored way
MLACLBIKA	BLACKMAIL	Get by threatening, coercing
ITLIUNJOBA	JUBILATION	A joyful celebration
SWETINS	WITNESS	Someone who signs a document to make it authentic

www.ingramcontent.com/pod-product-compliance
Lightning Source LLC
Chambersburg PA
CBHW051416070526
44584CB00023B/3448